Mini-Books are designed to
inform and entertain you.

They cover a wide range of
subjects—from Yoga to Cat-Care;
from Dieting to Dressmaking;
from Gardening to Antiques.

Mini-Books are neat
Mini-Books are cheap
Mini-Books are exciting

COLLECTING SILVER AND PLATE

is just one Mini-Book
from a choice of many.

Other Mini-Books by Guy Williams

Some further titles in the series—

GUY R. WILLIAMS

COLLECTING SILVER AND PLATE
(illustrated by the author)

A MINI-BOOK BY CORGI

COLLECTING SILVER AND PLATE

A MINI-BOOK   552 76361 6

PRINTING HISTORY

Mini-Book Edition published 1971
Copyright © 1971 Guy R. Williams

Mini-Books are published by Transworld Publishers Ltd.,
Cavendish House, 57–59 Uxbridge Road, Ealing,
London, W.5.
Filmset in Photon Times 10 pt. by
Richard Clay (The Chaucer Press), Ltd., Bungay, Suffolk
Printed in Great Britain by
Fletcher & Son Ltd., Norwich, Norfolk

CONTENTS

CHAPTER ONE

COLLECTING SILVER

Let us start at the very beginning. (It is unlikely that you will have picked up this book if you make a habit of bidding for valuable silver pieces at Christies' or Sotheby's or at one of the other important salerooms of the world. So we will assume that you would like to collect silver, but have not, yet, an extensive knowledge of this attractive metal.)

To call silver 'attractive' is, perhaps, to understate its peculiar qualities. Almost since prehistoric times it has been recognised, with gold, as a 'noble' metal. (At one stage, soon after it was first worked, it may even have been valued more highly than gold.) The Egyptians of the First Dynasty rated it a little less than half as valuable as gold. The Romans called it 'Argentum', and thought of it in the same terms as Luna the Moon, that pale, mysterious disc that lay beyond the reach of their imperial ambitions. In the Middle Ages gold was reckoned to be twenty times as valuable as silver. Today the relative values of gold and silver are nearer thirty and one. But, still, silver retains its unchallenged, undiminishing place in the affections of the houseproud and of all lovers of fine craftsmanship.

Pure silver is intensely white in colour, and it does not oxidise under any conditions. However, the metal is very little used in its pure form, as it is too soft to withstand for long any real wear and tear. Instead, it has always been the custom for metalworkers to make an alloy by mixing silver with copper. In this form it becomes an ideal material to work, combining strength, malleability and ductility in a remarkable degree, and having a finer, richer colour than the pure metal.

The proportions in which the silver and the copper may be mixed have been strictly controlled by law since the reign of King Edward I—an Act passed in A.D. 1300 laying down that the standard and approved mixture shall be 11 oz. 2 dwts. of pure silver to each 18 dwts. of copper—a standard that has been strictly enforced ever since, except during the critical years 1697–1719, when a higher standard (known as the 'Britannia' standard) was called for. In the Britannia standard, 230 parts of silver were—and, occasionally, still are—combined with 10 parts of copper. 'Britannia' silver is softer than 'Standard' silver, and can be 'raised' (that is, beaten up into a bowl shape from a flat sheet) more easily.

For almost as long as accurate records have been kept, pieces of silver have been collected for use, for display and to convey (without putting the message too ostentatiously into words) a vivid impression of the status and importance of their owners. So we find Samuel Pepys, the indefatigable Secretary of the Admiralty Board, writing in his diary in 1667:

> We had, with my wife and I, twelve at table, and a very good and pleasant company, and a most neat and excellent—but dear—dinner. But Lord! to see with what way they looked upon all my fine plate was pleasant; for I made the best show I could, to let them understand me and my condition, to take down the pride of Mrs. Clarke, who thinks herself very great.

During the eighteenth century the advantages of collecting pieces of silver became apparent to many people much farther down the social scale, and even comparatively modest homes were quite liberally furnished with the kind of cutlery and utensils that can be expected to fetch impressively high prices when they change hands today. By the time Queen Victoria had settled herself comfortably on her throne her wealthier subjects could only show off their exceptional good fortune by displays of an ostentatious vulgarity:

Hideous solidity was the characteristic of the Podsnap plate. Everything was made to look as heavy as it could and to take up as much room as possible. Everything said boastfully, 'Here you have as much of me in my ugliness as if I were only lead; but I am so many ounces of precious metal worth so much an ounce;—wouldn't you like to melt me down?' A corpulent straddling épergne, blotched all over as if it had broken out in an eruption rather than been ornamented, delivered this address from an unsightly silver platform in the centre of the table. Four silver wine-coolers, each furnished with four staring heads, each head obtrusively carrying a big silver ring in each of its ears, conveyed the sentiment up and down the table, and handed it on to the pot-bellied silver salt-cellars. All the big silver spoons and forks widened the mouths of the company expressly for the purpose of thrusting the sentiment down their throats with every morsel they ate.

Silver, when Charles Dickens wrote those words, was being raised in great quantities from the immense deposits of ore that had been newly discovered in America, Australia and elsewhere, so that by the end of the nineteenth century only the very poorest homes were without at least a few pieces of silver, even if these were brought out only on special occasions.

A silver entrée dish made with the elegant simplicity found in so much work of the 'Regency' period.

The collector of silver today, then, is offered a very wide range of choice. It is possible to form a collection of a few splendid eighteenth-century pieces only (the kind that are sometimes referred to, rather misleadingly, as 'ideal investments to beat inflation'), or, for the same outlay, to make a much more extensive collection of what we might call 'standard late Victorian domestic' with, perhaps, a few selected pieces from the present century thrown in for good measure. Either way lies a lot of pleasure and excitement.

We all love to own things—even a small child gets a special thrill when it uses the magic words 'It's mine!' This little book is intended to show you how you can give full rein to your collecting instincts in a field where the stakes tend to be high, and how, by acquiring a quota of desirable pieces of silver for your home, you can make it a pleasanter and more satisfying place to live in.

CHAPTER TWO

A FEW BASIC TERMS

There are just a few basic terms of which anyone intending to collect silver has to understand the meaning before he— or she—can operate at all. (There are many more that have to be defined before the beginner can operate with confidence in a field in which the expert will always have a distinct advantage over the amateur.) One or two of these basic terms have been used already in this book. They have had to wait to be explained.

Silver has always been measured by weight. (The Biblical terms 'shekel' and 'talent' refer directly to certain specific weights of a precious metal.) In 1526 'Troy Weight' was adopted as the official and legal measure in Britain—it had been introduced from Troyes, in France, a little more than a hundred years before—and it has been used ever since. The principal unit in Troy weight is the 'ounce' (there is no Troy pound!). Each Troy ounce is subdivided into twenty 'pennyweight', or '20 dwt.'. The pennyweight can be further subdivided into twenty-four grains, but this is not normally used for gold and silver.

With the move, in Britain, towards the wholesale adoption of the metric system, changes may be made in Troy weight. As this book is being compiled, no decisions have been announced.

It is possible to form a splendid collection of silver

without weighing a single piece, but if you are hoping to make money from your hobby instead of merely investing it, or forming a collection for pleasure alone, you will have to be prepared to learn how to use a balance—or a spring balance—reasonably accurately.

CHAPTER THREE

SILVER GILT

Another term that must be immediately defined is 'silver
gilt'. Much early silver was 'gilded', or given a thin coating
of gold that left it with a glorious, warm yellow patina, and
helped to protect it from the ill-effects of impurities in the
air. (See, later, a description of 'tarnishing'.) In some of
England's historic mansions there are separate strong-
rooms, still, for 'white' (or ungilded) silver, and 'gold' (that
is, gilded silver, NOT pure gold, which is found chiefly in
palaces).

To gild silver by the traditional method, gold had to be
dissolved in a mixture of sulphuric and nitric acids, and it
was then made into an amalgam with mercury. The piece of
silver that was to be gilded was then brought to a dull red
heat, and the amalgam was painted on to it. The mercury,
then, was driven off by the heat in the form of vapour,
leaving the gold to form an inseparable skin on the outer
surface of the silver. Unfortunately, the fumes produced by
this process were poisonous, and workers engaged for long
in the trade were virtually certain to sicken and die. So, by
the middle of the eighteenth century, the practice of gilding
silver had almost died out. It was revived during the nineteenth century, when safer techniques had been discovered
that involved the deposition of gold by electrolytic methods,
but the surfaces produced by the new process tend to be

overbright or crude in colour, and the older pieces are always preferred. Sometimes a piece would have the decorative parts only of its surface gilded, in which case it would be referred to as 'parcel gilt'. These pieces, if they are genuine, tend to be very valuable. A little less highly prized are the cups and other vessels that are gilt on the interior surfaces only. The correct trade term to use for these is (surprise, surprise) 'gilt inside'.

CHAPTER FOUR

HOW TO ACQUIRE SILVER

Buying silver is as fascinating—and as chancey—as any other form of collecting. 'The fool and his money are soon parted', said the old proverb, and it could with equal correctness have said, 'The silver-seeking fool and his money . . .'

But there are many people alive today who have formed splendid collections of silver that are worth, already, considerably greater sums than they have cost. These people have the pleasure of sitting to eat at tables that bring to mind Samuel Pepys' wish to 'have all things mighty rich and handsome about me'. And they know the joy of owning pieces that are, to any sensitive and appreciative eyes, as aesthetically satisfying as minor works of art.

They have invested their money, too, in objects of fine craftsmanship that will tend, over the years, to rise steadily in value as the number of similar pieces that can come on to the market steadily decreases. (Every year there is a certain amount of wastage, through fire loss and through burglaries——followed, so often, by surreptitious melting down. Museums, too, are constantly building up representative collections from which no first-rate items are ever likely to be released.) The rise in the market price of old silver pieces may be slowed down slightly during our rare periods of deflation, and the market may even suffer some shocks at times of serious financial crisis. But over the decades these set-backs may be seen to be rare. History shows that the value of good silver pieces tends, *in the long run*, to rise at a pace that more than compensates for these occasional hesitations. The value of an established and carefully chosen collection will, therefore, tend to increase most satisfactorily too.

Having decided that you would like to start collecting silver, you may possibly find yourself wondering when best, where best and how best to buy.

The answer to the first question is straightforward. It is: 'Begin as soon as you conveniently can.' Already, even the smaller late Victorian pieces that were produced in such great quantities for the homes of the prosperous middle classes are becoming scarcer. Soon they will be harder to find, and proportionately more expensive. So often one hears people say, 'I turned a piece like that down only a little time ago. Just look at the price of it now!' The go-ahead collector is not likely to feel such regret.

The second question—'Where is it best to buy silver?'—needs to be answered at much greater length. There is one prime factor to be considered: and that is the depth of your pocket.

Obviously, if you can afford to, you will go to one of the great dealers who specialise in fine silver pieces and whose names are almost household words. In their shops you will be given the closest and most sympathetic attention, you will be shown the most ravishing examples of the silversmith's craft, you will be able to rely on the descriptions you are given of these—and you will have to pay the full market price for what you are offered. It is not likely to be low. A Queen Anne coffee pot, purchased in this kind of setting would probably set you back at least £3,000!

If your means are more modest you may well choose to approach one or more of the smaller dealers who trade generally in antiques and the nicer household goods, and who handle only those pieces of silver that may come their way in the ordinary course of business. These dealers may not have the specialised knowledge of the more glamorous 'silver experts', but this does not necessarily mean that you are likely to find any remarkable bargains in their shops. Probably a dealer of this kind will have a very clear idea of the likely demand for any particular piece in his stock, and of the price he is likely to be able to get for it. He will not be a philanthropist. Still, many successful silver collectors have found that they have gained the best possible introduction to their pastime by getting to know one of these general traders. Approached frankly, such a man will usually treat you with fairness and sympathy. He knows that every new collector is, potentially, a regular customer.

If you are likely to enjoy hunting for treasure in less orthodox surroundings you may choose to pick your way through the mixture of junk and bric-à-brac, the genuine and the faked, the valuable and the virtually worthless, that is offered for sale in any popular 'antique market'. In London there are several of these. The market in the Caledonian Road, so famous in the days before the Second World War, is now—alas!—no more, but it has a worthy successor in the market held on Friday mornings in Bermondsey, near Tower Bridge. The market held in and around the Portobello Road is now thronged with visitors from all over the world. In Islington, around the Camden Passage, there is a charming little cluster of antique shops and booths, which are open all the week and are supplemented by a colourful open-air market as well on Saturdays. On Sundays, keen silver hunters wend their way to the busy little market held in Cutler Street, which is off Houndsditch, and is not far from the bustling Petticoat Lane. There are huddles of small shops, too—most of them very well and professionally run—in King's Road, Chelsea; in Kensington Church Street; in Heath Street, Hampstead; in Shepherd's Market, Mayfair; and in several of the 'suburban villages'. So, in the Metropolis at least, the silver hunter has plenty of opportunities for search. In Chancery Lane he—or she—can browse for hours in a positive Eldorado: the London Silver Vaults, which extend, under ground, over an excitingly wide area.

One of the most exciting methods of acquiring silver pieces for a collection is by bidding for them at public auctions. There are traps, here, for the unwary, but there are also many valuable lessons to be learned.

At auction sales held by firms such as Sothebys' and the other famous and important London houses, it is safe to rely on the descriptions given in the catalogues—these firms, careful of their reputations, employ staffs of experts to make sure that you can. In the smaller provincial salerooms you may have to be more cautious. There, the catalogues—drawn up, possibly, by well-meaning enthusiasts who have had no extended specialist training—may be entirely misleading. And if you examine closely the 'Conditions of Sale' (printed, usually, on the first or last page of the catalogue) you will almost certainly find that each lot is offered on the understanding that it will be sold at the purchaser's own risk—that is, the auctioneer is disclaiming all responsibility. 'Caveat Emptor', runs the old Latin tag. Let the buyer beware!

Assuming, then, that you are willing to back your own

judgement, you will have to follow certain recognised procedures. If the saleroom is crowded, stand where you can get a good view of the auctioneer, thereby making sure that he will be able to see you. You can safely assume that a large proportion of those present will be there merely from motives of curiosity, and may have no intention of making a single bid. So, as a lot you are interested in approaches, don't feel that you are being rude or boorish if you make your way discreetly but firmly to a better strategic position.

When you bid, bid quickly, so that you do not draw an undue amount of attention to yourself. Once the auctioneer knows you are bidding, it will usually be sufficient for you to make a small gesture with your head, an unobtrusive movement of your catalogue, or an indication with your finger that you wish to remain 'in the running'.

Many auctioneers are skilled at inducing inexperienced collectors to bid more than they have intended. (It is a wise precaution, always, to decide before the bidding begins what the maximum amount is that you would be willing to pay for each lot you would like to purchase.) Usually, these 'raising tactics' consist of rushing out the bids, so that an atmosphere of emotional tension is generated. Occasionally, an unscrupulous auctioneer may try to urge a bidder on to higher levels by appealing to him publicly. ('Surely you're not dropping out now, sir?' is a favourite gambit, with its suggestion that the bidder is faint-hearted, or short on resources.) When this happens, write on a piece of paper 'Please take my bids as confidential', and ask one of the porters to give it to the auctioneer. Then you should not suffer this embarrassment again.

It is inadvisable to make a bid for any lot on the spur of the moment. (You should examine carefully, and at leisure, before the auction begins, any piece in which you are at all interested.) Once you have made a bid, it is made, and cannot normally be retracted. When you have decided to stop bidding, make that fact known to the auctioneer with a firm shake of the head, and do not be tempted to join in again. Should you dispute the outcome of any auction, you may well lose the good will of the auctioneer and his assistants, so that it will be difficult for you to bid successfully in that saleroom again. For this reason it is important to be quite clear in your own mind about which lot you are actually bidding for. It can be disconcerting to find that while you have been bidding keenly for, say, a silver salver you want badly, your principal competitors, and the auctioneer, have been trying to decide the future ownership of, say, some late Victorian monstrosity to which you would not willingly give houseroom.

One major pitfall may be encountered in auctions of fine silver: not infrequently the lots are bid for, and sold, 'per ounce'—that is, the price quoted has to be multiplied by the weight of the piece, measured in ounces, to establish the amount of money that will actually have to be paid by the purchaser. To take a simple example: a silver teapot, weighing 20 oz., may be knocked down at £15. The purchaser, then, would have to find £300. In some cases—as, for example, in a coffee pot with an ivory handle—an allowance would be made for the estimated weight of the ivory.

CHAPTER FIVE

THE TECHNIQUES OF THE SILVERSMITH

It is not very likely that many collectors of fine silver, today, will be sufficiently enthusiastic to try working in silver themselves. Life is too short, most people would say, to study any subject, however fascinating, in such depth. But it may pay you to learn a little, at least, about the traditional techniques of the silversmith before you spend too much money on the objects of your fancy. The silversmith's methods have hardly changed since the craft was developed in the mysterious centuries that preceded the birth of Christ. Even in the time of the Pharaohs, rude lathes were used for turning and spinning silver. Stamping with dies may be almost as old. Anyone who studies and understands these techniques—and the other, more sophisticated techniques of the present-day silversmith—will inevitably appreciate many qualities in the pieces in his (or her) collection that would otherwise have escaped notice. Here is a very brief survey of some of the silversmith's traditional methods. For more detailed reading you should consult the books recommended in the list on page 124.

(a) THE RAW MATERIAL

Silver is normally bought from the refiner in sheet form, or as wire. Before any suitable form of machinery had been invented, sheet silver had to be beaten out by hand (a highly tedious process, you will appreciate, that left undesirable hammer marks). Then, in 1727, John Cook took out a patent to protect his ingenious 'flatting mill'. With this machine, which was not fully exploited until the patent had run out a little later in the century, sheet silver was produced by passing the raw material through a series of rollers, any tendency that the silver may have had to become brittle in the process being counteracted by frequent annealing. Cook's mill made it possible for sheet silver to be produced rapidly and reliably by workers who were not fully trained craftsmen. The sheets produced were perfectly flat and smooth and did not have to have hammer marks removed from them as did, inevitably, the sheets produced previously by hand.

Soon after the rolling mill was developed, further machines were designed that produced decorative borders, in long strips, with (to take only one example) the popular 'gadroon' or 'piecrust' pattern impressed upon them. These ready-made edges quickly found favour with the craftsmen who resented the time they had had to spend previously in producing such fashionable embellishments laboriously, by hand. Matthew Boulton, of Birmingham, was one of the great innovators in this direction. At his London warehouse the silversmiths of the Metropolis were able to purchase his ready-rolled borders, as well as ready-cast handles and legs. By soldering these to simple bodies of standard designs, the London men were able to produce and market desirable goods at fiercely competitive rates. Stamped at Goldsmiths' Hall with the appropriate marks, these pieces pass now as authentic examples of the eighteenth-century silversmiths' craft. It is only the collector with heightened sensibilities who, without being previously 'briefed', can tell the difference between one of these sophisticated commercial productions and an earlier, hand-worked masterpiece. (Literally, '*Master* piece'.) By the time you have been handling Georgian (and earlier) silver for a year or two, your feeling for fine craftsmanship should have developed to the point where you can distinguish, at a glance, between a competently fabricated job that has been mass-produced for sale at a reasonably low price in the everyday domestic market, and a piece that has been designed and produced on a 'one off only' basis.

(*b*) RAISING

A flat piece of silver sheet can be 'raised' so that it forms a curved, bowl shape quite easily—it has to be held against a suitable 'former', or 'head', and struck with a wooden mallet until the metal takes the form that the craftsman wishes it to take. An inexperienced worker will hit the metal so hard and carelessly that it will be marred by deep folds and wrinkles. The operation in which the surface of the silver is smoothed with a flat-faced hammer is known as 'planishing.'

(*c*) SPINNING

This is the name given to the process by which sheet silver can be shaped on a power-driven lathe by being forced with highly polished steel burnishers on to a former that has been previously turned from hard wood. Many modern silver cups and bowls are 'spun' in this way.

(d) SOLDERING

From the earliest days of metal-working, men have known that pieces of silver can be joined securely and unobtrusively if a suitable alloy is made that will be:

(i) more easily fused (that is, 'melted') than silver itself;

(ii) not noticeably different from silver in strength or colour.

By melting such an alloy and by allowing it to flow along and into the joint, the process known generally as 'soldering' is carried out. Certain materials known as 'fluxes' are used to help the melted solder to flow easily over and into the places where it is most needed.

Soldering has to be carried out by the silversmith with extreme care and cleanliness. Silver solders normally contain zinc, which is readily attacked by any acid that may be accidentally brought into contact with it. Other metals, such as tin and lead, are liable to damage a fine silver surface almost irreparably if they are allowed to come into contact with it when they are in a fused state. The perfection of the work carried out by the greatest craftsmen is a splendid testimony to their meticulousness.

(e) CASTING

Many of the more intricate or decorative parts of the silver pieces we collect will have been 'cast' by the silversmith, or by some specialist who has been prepared to do this work for him.

A traditional method of casting involves the preparation of a preliminary model of each separate part that is to be

25

cast. For making these models, wax may be used—wax that has been softened by being warmed. Plaster of Paris is normally used for making the necessary moulds from the pattern or prototype. When the pattern is removed from the moulds its place is taken by melted silver, which then conforms to the desired shape. (The process is not quite as simple as it is made to sound here. To describe it fully would take many pages.) An elaborate piece, such as a silver Victorian table decoration, may have dozens of castings soldered to it, to produce an almost overwhelming effect.

(f) EMBOSSING

Embossing (sometimes referred to as 'Repoussé work') is the art of raising ornament in relief where pressure is applied from the reverse side of the metal. Normally, the design is drawn on the surface of the metal—in our case, silver—in such a way that the outlines are visible on the back of the work. The work is then placed face downwards on a pitch or asphalt block, and the portions to be raised are hammered down with special tools into the relatively soft support. Next, the work is reversed, and the background or 'depressed' shapes are hammered down into the pitch.

(g) CHASING

This is a technique in which the silversmith works on the surface of the metal with a hammer and a number of different, specially designed, punches, to produce a wide variety of decorative effects. Sometimes parts of a silver surface will be beaten down to form a depressed background to other parts that are to remain 'in relief'.

It is quite usual to find silver pieces in which parts have

been chased, as well as embossed. The two techniques are complementary: most embossed work is given its final sharpness, or detail, by the application of a chasing tool.

(*h*) ENGRAVING

This is a technique that involves the cutting or incising of a line or lines in the surface of a piece of silver. It is carried out with a specially designed cutting tool, usually by pressure from the craftsman's hand. (When a hammer has to be used to provide the pressure, the process is usually referred to as 'carving'.)

Many pieces of silver plate produced in the eighteenth and early nineteenth centuries are beautifully engraved—often, with elaborate heraldic designs. It is instructive to remmember that William Hogarth (1697–1764), one of Britain's most honoured artists, learned his job by being apprenticed, in London, to Ellis Gamble, an 'engraver of arms on silver plate', who had his establishment in 'Cranbourne Street or Alley near Leicester Fields' (now Leicester Square). It is not beyond the bounds of possibility that there are on the market even today a number of pieces that passed through Gamble's hands and were engraved by his talented apprentice.

(*i*) CUT CARD WORK

This is a technique introduced into Britain by silver-smiths from France late in the seventeenth century. The craftsman using this method of ornamenting a piece of silver plate would cut the decorations from sheet silver, and he would then fix them firmly into position with silver solder surface to be embellished. It was a method that

27

quickly became popular with English and Irish silversmiths because the addition of an extra thickness of silver—even if it were only a band of formalised leaves—tended to increase the strength of the work, as well as making it appreciably richer in appearance.

(*j*) PIERCING

During the second half of the eighteenth century pierced silver work became fashionable in a number of different styles, and cake baskets and bread baskets, mustard pots, decanter stands and other small useful domestic articles were turned out in great profusion—so much so that some most decorative examples are still well within the reach of collectors of moderate means.

The drill was—it is believed—one of the earliest tools ever to have been devised by man. It is not surprising, then, that the first holes to be pierced for decorative purposes in sheet silver are said to have been made with simple drills. The chisel was introduced into the silversmith's shop a little later. (Chisel-cut pierced work is often extremely beautiful, but this was an extremely laborious process, and called for great skill.)

After that it became usual for holes to be made with drills of various sizes, the remaining surplus metal being removed with very small files.

When metal-workers had discovered how to make small saws of steel wire, the 'piercing saw' was added to the silversmith's equipment, and swifter techniques were evolved. With the coming of mass-production processes, even hand-saw piercing proved to be too slow and expensive, except for work of the very highest quality, and most repetitive piercing (sometimes classical, sometimes in the

'Chinoiserie' style) was done by mechanically operated presses. The making of the necessary press tools was regarded as a trade in itself.

Pierced work usually appears at its best and richest when the silver is seen against the backing of a dark blue glass liner.

CHAPTER SIX

THE PENDULUM OF TASTE

Fashions in silver plate have tended to change at more or less regular intervals, just as modes change in clothes, in hair styles and in ways of living. The greatest period of English silver—extending, approximately, from 1678 to 1830—was notable for several of these vogues. Two or three terms used with reference to these may also need to be explained.

(*a*) BAROQUE

The word 'Baroque' is often applied by dealers and collectors to pieces made in the early eighteenth century under the influence of Lord Burlington and his 'tame' architect and designer William Kent. The formal but decorative appearance of these is derived from the 'Palladian' style, originating in Italy, that was favoured by Burlington and Kent.

(*b*) ROCOCO

This is the name applied freely to a more playful style that also came into fashion early in the eighteenth century. It was a time when social gatherings of all kinds were the rage—in London and the fashionable spas, balls, dinner, tea and breakfast parties, assemblies, receptions and routs filled the leisure hours of most members of the landed and monied classes. To provide appropriately gay and decorative settings for these enjoyable occasions, architects, furniture makers and silversmiths developed, under French influence, a less austere style than the 'Baroque' style just mentioned. The new style was highly ornamental, and pieces executed in it can be immediately recognised by the profuse application of scrolls, shells, scales, swirling foliage and other luxurious motifs. Designers working in the Rococo manner were usually eager to soften or disguise the straight lines in their work (curves were so much less *severe*) and they were prepared, too, to introduce many asymmetrical elements. Even a formal coat-of-arms, bespoken by the owner of a piece of plate, would probably be framed in an extravagant 'freehand' cartouche or frame.

(c) CHINOISERIE

With tea and other exotic imports coming from the Orient, it is not surprising that silversmiths and other craftsmen of the late seventeenth and eighteenth centuries should look to the ancient civilisations of the East for much of their inspiration. The style known as 'Chinoiserie' is a delightful demonstration of this preoccupation with remote and romantic regions. Frequently, one will find—say—a silver tea caddy decorated richly with raised Chinese figures or scenes.

CHAPTER SEVEN

HALL-MARKS

Collecting silver is unlike any other form of collecting, in that all pieces—with a few exceptions, to be described later —carry with them some precise information about where and when they were made (and, in the case of many pieces made after the end of the seventeenth century, they may carry some information about the identity of the maker, too). Collectors of china and pewter are accustomed to studying the marks on the pieces they acquire, or are considering for purchase (if any are present), but the marks on these objects differ in one very important respect from those to be found on silver—they are just the potters' or pewterers' marks, arbitrarily chosen, and are not officially regulated. The hall-marking of silver, on the other hand, has been strictly controlled by Act of Parliament since the Middle Ages, and has been carried out under the direct supervision of the most responsible authorities. Interference with the legal process of hall-marking has always been regarded as a felony and at one time was a capital crime. (As recently as 1815 an Act of Parliament was passed making the counterfeiting of the Duty Mark—at that time, the king's head—a crime punishable by death. The duty levied then on silver plate was 1s. 6d. per ounce.)

It would be impossible to include in a book of this length complete tables of the hall-marks and annual date letters employed in the various assay offices, but comprehensive information about these is available now in some excellent handbooks, and the acquisition of one of these is recommended to anyone who intends to collect silver seriously. [For details of some of the best, see the Suggestions for Further Reading on page 124.] In this section you will find only some general notes about the subject that will explain at least what the marks on your silver pieces represent, and how they came to be there.

THE ORIGINS OF THE MARKS

As early as the year 1238 the Mayor and Aldermen of the City of London decided to appoint a committee of six honourable men who were to see that no gold or silver pieces should be made with metal that was inferior to that of the coinage. By the end of that century the 'Mistery' or Company of Goldsmiths had been properly organised, the method of testing or 'assay' had been determined and the mark had been chosen that was to be used on all metal that came up to the required standard. This mark was the leopard's head ('Une teste de leopart', it was called in the Norman-French language of heraldry. To all intents and purposes the head shown is that of a lion—one of the lions *passant guardant* of the Royal Arms, and it is therefore a royal mark.)

From 1300 to 1363 this mark was used alone, unless a maker chose to add (quite voluntarily) his personal mark. Then, in the latter year, a Statute of King Edward III decreed that 'every goldsmith should have a mark by himself, for which he should answer, to be struck beside the King's mark.' For a few decades this mark would normally be some personal sign or symbol that could be clearly

33

recognised—possibly the sign that stood as a trade-mark over the master's workshop. Later the goldsmith's (or silversmith's) initials were added to, or substituted for, the sign, but in spite of this it is extremely difficult to identify the work of any individual silversmith that was assayed before the year 1697. In 1697 it became compulsory for all craftsmen in silver to mark their work with the first two letters of their surname, and their marks were registered—to avoid further confusion—at the Goldsmiths' Hall. In 1719 this Act was repealed, and during the period 1720–39 many silversmiths began to mark their work once again with the initials of their Christian name and surname, creating a right old muddle. In 1739 the situation was finally clarified when the makers were ordered to destroy all existing punches and to register new ones, in which their ordinary initials were to be used, of an entirely different type from those they had used before.

The date-mark, or as it is sometimes called, 'the assayer's mark', is a letter of the alphabet that is stamped on a piece of silver with the express purpose of indicating the year in which that piece was presented for assay. The earliest date letters were used in 1478, and since that time complete records have been kept of the London practice. (The date letters used at the various provincial assay centres, though a little more haphazard, are also known.) Clearly, since there are only twenty-six letters in the alphabet (and in London the letters J, W, X, Y and Z have not been used) a change has had to be made in the style of the letters used each time the cycle has been recommenced. Since 1560 the letters have been enclosed in heraldic shields of varying shapes, and the differences between these, combined with the different types of letters used, has made it easier to tell, by a quick look at a reference book, the year of assay.

THE LION 'PASSANT'

No one knows for certain how the lion *passant* came to appear on English silver, for though it has been found on plate that dates from the middle of the sixteenth century, no mention of it was made in the records of the Goldsmiths' Company (as far as can now be discovered) until 1597. Possibly the appearance of the lion in 1544 or 1545 is connected with the successive debasements of the currency carried out by Henry VIII about that time. Previously, as we have seen, the leopard's head had been used to denote silver that was in no way inferior to that of the coin of the realm. Probably when the coin of the realm itself became inferior, the Wardens of the Goldsmiths' Company decided to put an additional mark on all silver plate that came up to their required standards, to show that it had not been made from debased metal. At various times the lion *passant* has been enclosed in a number of different outlines—from 1678 to 1697, for instance, it was shown in a cartouche with a flat base:

and from about 1784 to 1822 in a regular shield of heraldic shape:

These changes are recorded in 'Chaffer's Handbook to Hall Marks on Gold and Silver Plate' and other books of reference, and assist us, with the other guides, to determine the date of our silver.

THE PROVINCIAL CENTRES

In the year 1723 seven cities were appointed by a Statute of King Henry VI to exercise (in addition to London) the right of assaying gold and silver plate. The new centres were Salisbury and Bristol (for the West Country), Lincoln and Norwich (for the East), Coventry (for the Midlands) and Newcastle and York (for what are now the Northern Counties). York, Newcastle and Norwich eventually adopted town marks of their own—York, a half leopard's head combined with a half fleur-de-lis, changed after 1700 to a shield on a cross, showing five lions *passant guardant*; Newcastle, one or three castles on shields of varying shapes; Norwich, a castle and lion, or a rose crowned. London, which continued to function as the principal centre, continued to use the leopard's head alone as a town mark—

possibly because the goldsmiths and silversmiths there felt they had a prior claim to it.

The history of the provincial assaying centres is too ill-documented and confusing to be of very much interest to the average collector, but there are, as has been said, some very informative guides that will help the specialist in his researches. By 1700 Lincoln, Salisbury and Coventry had ceased to assay silver. In 1700–1 an Act of Parliament re-appointed Bristol, Norwich and York, and in 1701–2 Newcastle was re-appointed and Exeter and Chester were added to the list. Birmingham and Sheffield were appointed in 1773. (Plate made in Birmingham prior to 1773 would have had to be sent to London or Chester for assay, and it will, therefore, bear no mark that immediately associates it with Birmingham. This is fairly typical of the difficulties that one may encounter when one is trying to identify pieces of plate!)

This shows how the hall-marks on a piece of English provincial silver can tell the collector much about the origins of that piece. These punch marks show (left to right) the initials of the maker; the lion *passant guardant* and the leopard's head crowned (the attestations of the quality of the silver); the town mark of Chester; and the date letter 'H', which shows that the piece was assayed in the year 1733/4.

THE BRITANNIA MARK

In 1697 an Act of Parliament was passed that has been mentioned earlier in this book. This Act called for a higher standard of purity in silver than had been demanded previously, and new marks were instituted that were to take the place of the leopard's head and the lion *passant*. The marks used for the new, purer silver were to be 'a lion's head erased' and 'the figure of a woman commonly called Britannia'. For twenty-two years Britannia ruled supreme. Then in 1719 silver of the old standard was allowed once again, and the old marks came back into use. But the Britannia's mark with the lion's head erased has continued to be used, since then, for silver produced voluntarily to conform to the higher standard.

THE SOVEREIGN'S HEAD

A mark on a piece of silver that shows the head of a reigning sovereign in profile indicates that duty has been paid on that piece, according to law. The duty, which was collected by the officers of the Goldsmiths' Company, who were officially appointed to receive it, was first levied in England and Scotland in 1719, when the old silver standard was revived. In 1730 the duty was also imposed on silver plate assayed in Ireland, and from this date on the figure of Hibernia was used on Irish plate to show that the duty had been properly paid. By an Act passed in 1784 (that is, in the reign of George III) it was determined that English and Scottish silver, too, should be marked appropriately when the levy had been paid. So from St. Dunstan's Day (19th May) 1784, when the new legislation first took effect, the king's head (or in the case of Victoria, the queen's head) was shown on all properly paid-up plate.

At first George III's head was shown facing towards the left. From 1786 onwards, however, he was shown facing towards the right and so too, in their turn, were the succeeding sovereigns George IV (1820–June 1831) and William

IV (to June 1837). Queen Victoria, however, is shown facing left again. The sovereign's head mark continued to be used until the year 1890, when this particular duty was abolished.

THE MARK FOR FOREIGN PLATE

This mark, called for by an Act of 1876 and an Order in Council made in 1904, concerns only silver imported from abroad and is of little concern to the average collector.

EXCEPTIONS TO THE MARKING LAWS

Occasionally you may find a small silver article that does not appear to have been hall-marked. This may be a piece that has been 'excused' or 'exempted'. By an Act passed in 1738, for example, certain small pieces were made exempt either on account of their size, or because their appearance would be spoiled by the addition of hall-marks. Among these were buttons, buckles, lockets, thimbles, the mounts and stoppers of glass bottles, and various trinkets. A later Act revised the list. Of course, many silver articles were presented for assay, and stamped when found to be up to the required standard, even though they were technically exempt.

*   *   *

Though no one who collects silver seriously today can afford to ignore the marks stamped upon the pieces in his possession, there was a time—and not so very long ago—when no one outside the trade seems to have realised their importance. Even as late as 1852 a Mr. Octavius Morgan, who pioneered the study of hall-marks, was able to write:

Every person who is possessed of an article of gold or silver plate has most probably observed a small group of marks stamped on some part of it. Few however have, I believe, regarded them in any other light than as a proof that the article so marked is made of the metal which it professes to be, and that the metal itself is of a certain purity . . .

The 'Mistery' of Goldsmiths had indeed remained mysterious to the members of the lay public for close on six hundred years. It was largely due to the researches of Octavius Morgan that so much is now generally known about this most interesting subject.

CHAPTER EIGHT

HOW THE FAKER WORKS

Although the hall-marks on a piece of old silver are, in effect, a guarantee of its authenticity, the collector will occasionally come across a piece that has been 'tampered with' by some dishonest and unscrupulous person. (It is 'occasionally', too. The heavy punishments that have been traditionally imposed on those tempted to counterfeit assay marks have acted as most salutary deterrents.)

If there is any doubt at all about the genuineness of a piece of silver, it is always advisable to have a close look through a powerful magnifying glass at the general surroundings of the hall-marks. The most usual expedient of the counterfeiter is known usually as 'letting in'. This entails cutting out the assay marks and date letter from a genuine old piece of silver that has relatively little value (probably it will be a small piece of no great distinction, such as an ordinary domestic spoon) and letting them into a very much larger piece that may be a modern reproduction. This is usually done so skilfully that the 'scars' of the dishonest insertion will not be readily seen by the naked eye. Some tell-tale irregularities of the surface will probably be apparent, though, if it is submitted to the closer inspection recommended above.

CHAPTER NINE

COLLECTING SILVER SPOONS

To be born with a silver spoon in one's mouth is, pro-
verbially, the sign that one is to be associated with great
wealth. But one does not have to be abnormally rich to have
the pleasure of eating with real silver spoons—even, for that
matter, with beautifully made eighteenth-century spoons
that have survived from that period of great elegance. So, if
you have not yet started to collect silver, but are considering
doing so, there is a lot to be said for taking spoons as your
first items of research. Even the addition of a single
Georgian teaspoon to your table is liable to send you out
looking keenly for more.

The earliest silver spoons found in Britain are at least
twelve hundred years old. You are not very likely to
encounter any as venerable as this outside museums, nor,
unless you are very wealthy, are you likely to be offered any
genuine examples of the 'Apostle' spoons that were so
popular in the reigns of Queen Elizabeth I and Kings James
I and Charles I. These had 'knops' or handle-ends made to
represent the twelve Apostles with their Master, each being
able to be identified by the personal emblem he carried: St.
Bartholomew, for instance, carried a butcher's knife; St.
Peter, the key of Heaven or a fish; St. Thomas, a spear or a
carpenter's square; St. Matthew (usually) a purse or wallet;
St. Simon Zelotes, a long saw; and St. Andrew the saltire

cross that is always associated with him.

In Tudor and early Stuart times it was the custom to offer sets of these Apostle spoons as christening gifts. (God-parents who were insufficiently wealthy had to content themselves with offering a single spoon, or, perhaps, the four that represented the Evangelists.) In Shakespeare's 'Famous History of the Life of King Henry the Eighth', we find Archbishop Cranmer—after he has protested that, being merely a humble subject, he is unworthy to act as a sponsor—earning this reproach from the King:

'Come, come, my Lord, you'ld spare your spoons.'

Many of these spoons that had been the treasured posses-sions of their owners were melted down, with so much other plate, to pay for the enormous expenses of the Civil War. (In 1642, for example, the loyal Royalists in the north of England were taking their silver to the King at York, while in London the citizens were similarly supporting the parlia-mentarians, even with women's thimbles. Only a tiny frac-tion of the silverware of England survived this holocaust.) Most of the Apostle spoons that did survive had their saints cut off once the Puritans, who saw in them reminders of 'idolatry', came to power at the end of the Civil War.

The earliest spoons the normal silver collector is likely to be even remotely concerned with are the 'Trifid' spoons that became fashionable soon after the Restoration. These had their handles flattened at the ends, the flattened metal being trimmed into the shape of a trefoil. 'Rat tail' spoons may be occasionally found, too, that date from the end of the seven-teenth century. These get their name from the tapering 'tail' of silver that was added, to strengthen each spoon, at the

43

junction of its bowl and handle, and extended along the back of the bowl.

The great influx of silversmiths into England from France after Louis XIV repealed the Edict of Nantes in 1685 was largely responsible for the splendid era of English silver that lasted for nearly a century. The names of many of these highly skilled refugees—Garnier, Harache, Mettayer, Platel and (in a following wave) Paul de Lamerie, to cite only a few—are well known to collectors today. Other immigrants, forced by their penurious circumstances to work for little more than a mere pittance, sold their products to London makers who took their purchases to Goldsmiths' Hall and had them assayed and hall-marked as their own.

During the decades that followed the Restoration and the Revocation of the Edict of Nantes, there was at first a serious shortage of the metal needed for the growing industry. Silver coins were quietly withdrawn from circulation and melted down, until the shortage of currency led the Grand Jury of Middlesex to petition the Crown to forbid the use of silver for tankards and other vessels in taverns. Only innkeepers were to be allowed to have silver spoons! Even the coins that were saved from the melting pot were liable to be illegally trimmed:

> Hundreds of wretched persons were dragged up Holborn Hill [says Arthur Hayden, in his invaluable book *Chats on Old Silver*], and in spite of flogging, branding, and hanging, the trade of the coin clipper was easier than highway robbery, and as fortunes were to be made those who followed that avocation took the risk, as did smugglers. It was a dangerous occupation. Seven men were hanged one morning and a woman branded, but this

44

did not deter the hundreds who were undetected. One clipper who was caught offered £6,000 for a pardon, which was rejected, but the news gave a stimulus to the industry.

Whoever was found in the possession of silver clippings, filings or parings (said the Government) should be burned in the cheek with a red-hot iron. Later, when silver was imported more plentifully from Latin America and other sources, English and Huguenot silversmiths alike were able to increase their output significantly.

Having more silver with which to experiment, the silversmiths catering for the fashion-conscious upper and middle classes during the remainder of the eighteenth century were able to evolve spoons in a tantalising variety of styles. Common to all of these, however, is a new outline of the stem or handle—shaped in a curve without a break—that has continued right up to the present day. The collector with limited resources can still find excellent examples of eighteenth-century London and provincial work at prices well within his reach, though clearly he will have to pay much more for spoons in matched sets than he will for the single odd example. (But even an individual spoon may have some quaintness or charm. An eighteenth-century silver teaspoon acquired for a few shillings for the author's collection had certain indentations in the bowl that puzzled him, until he discovered, quite by chance, that this spoon had been used on a Worcestershire farm during the reign of Queen Victoria for feeding the farmer's orphan or 'tiddling' lambs. The indentations had been honourably gained.)

From the middle of the eighteenth century onwards, for three or four decades, there was a great demand for silver 'caddy spoons', to be used for taking the precious tea leaves from the containers in which they were stored, and for measuring them before they went into the pot. Many most interesting collections of caddy spoons have been made, but unfortunately this is one of the branches of the silver craft that has more, perhaps, than others attracted the attention of the skilful faker. 'Caveat emptor', once more.

At this stage it may be interesting to notice the varying positions in which hall-marks may be found in seventeenth- and eighteenth-century silver spoons.

Until 1660, and for some years afterwards, a leopard's head would usually be stamped inside the bowl, the rest of the marks being found on the handle. After the reign of Charles II the marks would usually appear on the handle, close to the bowl. After the year 1781, or thereabouts, the marks were usually placed near the end of the handle. In a great many spoons that have been in regular domestic use, consistent over-enthusiastic polishing will have virtually erased the hall-marks or, at least, rendered them almost indecipherable. Where this has happened, the position of the marks may offer, at least, some rough guide to the age of the spoon.

Early in Queen Victoria's reign, spoons that are referred to now as 'Queen's pattern' were produced. Each of these was decorated with a shell, at the base of the bowl, and had raised lines that formed decorative borders to its shank. These spoons may not have been as supremely elegant as those produced in the Georgian period, but they are pleasant to look at, and pleasant to handle, and are not unreasonably expensive.

CHAPTER TEN

COLLECTING SILVER COFFEE POTS
AND CHOCOLATE POTS

A wealthy man who wished to own one superlative example of the silversmith's craft, and one only, would probably choose a silver coffee pot made by one of the best-known masters of the eighteenth century, such as Samuel Wastell, Hester Bateman or Paul de Lamerie. The more modestly endowed person who is starting to collect domestic silver may have to wait a very long time before such a treasure comes within his (or her) reach, but he (or she) will become more aware of the supreme beauties of the finest silver if some of the best examples of these utilitarian vessels—and many are on view in the great public museums—are carefully studied.

Coffee, today, is drunk as readily by women as by men, but there was a time when this beverage aroused strong female prejudices. In 1674 a petition was presented to Parliament by a numerous body of the fair sex. It alleged that coffee

> made men as unfruitful as the deserts whence that unhappy berry is said to be brought; that the offspring of our mighty ancestors would dwindle into a succession of apes and pygmies, and on a domestic message, a husband would stop by the way to drink a couple of cups of coffee.

Unlike silver teapots that were produced during the late seventeenth and eighteenth centuries in a number of different forms, coffee pots tended to remain, basically, very

Two seventeenth-century silver coffee pots of great elegance.

much as they had begun—that is, tall, rather than compact; and resembling, usually, truncated (that is, 'beheaded') cones or enlarged raindrops. Very occasionally, silver coffee pots may be found that have their handles at the sides, but more often the handles are set exactly opposite to the spouts, and are generally made from ebony or ivory.

It is for the unequalled elegance of their form that we value eighteenth-century silver coffee pots so highly. Every part of a first-rate example will be a delight to look at—the spout, made possibly to resemble the head and neck of a dragon, so that the coffee appears from the beast's open mouth; the lid, beautifully hinged, and made to be lifted by the lightest of touches on a finial that may be shaped, with a nice touch of humour, like an acorn or pineapple; the handle—mentioned already above—that is designed in a series of broken curves so that it is at the same time practical and playful; and finally the wide foot, on which the coffee pot rests with such delicacy and such assurance. Rarely have the functional and the aesthetically satisfying been so happily married.

The best eighteenth-century silver coffee pots, then, can always be relied on to command exceptionally high prices when they appear in the salerooms. (As this book is being compiled, Queen Anne coffee pots are fetching over £3,000, and fine examples by later Georgian silversmiths such as Thomas Whipman are changing hands at prices between £700 and £1,800. Even a pot made in the reign of George IV may cost as much as £350 to £450). But even with these prices to tempt one it is dangerous to regard antique silver as a foolproof investment. Market prices can go down just as quickly as they can go up. 'It's much easier to buy the wrong thing than to buy the right thing', warned a spokesman for a well-known firm of silver dealers during a recent credit squeeze. 'The frantic boom over the past year has meant that people who know nothing have been buying terrible things. Six months ago a fine Georgian coffee pot would sell for say £1,800, a poor one for perhaps £1,500. Now the good pot might just fetch the same price, but the poor one would only make perhaps £800. The first things to fall in price are the second-rate objects.'

Chocolate is a beverage that has only a limited appeal today, but in the reigns of Charles II and James II it was regarded as a very choice luxury. There is reason to believe that the earliest silver coffee pots were intended to be used (on suitable occasions) for serving chocolate instead of coffee. It is sometimes possible to spot one of these 'dual purpose' pots if one looks for an aperture in the lid through which a rod would have been inserted for stirring the contents. In some pots, this hole was concealed by the finial or knob on top of the lid. The knob, in these cases, had to be unscrewed before the stirring could begin. Other pots may have been made especially for chocolate. Chocolate drinking became steadily less fashionable as the eighteenth century drew towards its close. By the beginning of Queen Victoria's reign it was popular only with a small minority.

CHAPTER ELEVEN

COLLECTING SILVER TEAPOTS

For more than three centuries British men and women have found some consolation for the rigours of our climate by drinking tea. 'The cup that cheers but does not inebriate' is still, today, one of the most popular national beverages. It follows, then, that whole books—and lengthy ones—can be written on the subject of teapots alone.

As early as 1660 the great diarist Samuel Pepys was recording his impressions of the newly introduced form of refreshment. Ten years later a fine silver teapot, now in the Victoria and Albert Museum at South Kensington, changed hands. It was inscribed:

> This Silver tea Pott was presented to ye Com^ttee of ye East India Company by ye Right Hono^le George Lord Berkeley of Berkeley Castle. A member of that Honourable and worthy Society and A true Hearty Louer of them. 1670.

The pot—shaped as a truncated cone with a conical lid, so that it looks remarkably like a lantern of that period—was engraved with the arms of Lord Berkeley and those of the East India Company. The date letter and hall-marks on the pot show that it was assayed in London in the year that it left the hands of the 'Hearty Louer'.

It is difficult for us to appreciate today how great a

luxury tea was, when the leaves were first brought halfway across the world to our shores. The price of tea, when Pepys first sampled the beverage, was 60s. per pound (equivalent to a great deal more, at present-day values). It was not much cheaper when Thomas Garway, retailer of tobacco and coffee, first offered tea over the counter to his customers. This is how Garway advertised the new, exciting commodity:

Tea in England hath been sold in the leaf for six pounds, and sometimes for ten pounds the pound weight, and in respect of its former scarceness and dearness it hath been only used as a regalia in high treatments and entertainments, and presents made thereof to princes and grandees till the year 1657. The said Garway did purchase a quantity thereof, the first publicly sold the said tea in leaf or drink, made according to the directions of the most knowing merchants into those Eastern countries. On the knowledge of the said Garway's continued care and industry in obtaining the best tea, and making drink thereof, very many noblemen, physicians, merchants, etc., have resort to his house to drink the drink thereof. He sells tea from 16s. to 50s. a pound.

During the early years of the eighteenth century silver teapots were made less and less like the tall, conical coffee pots of the time, until at last they took the forms (generally speaking) that we know so well today. During the reign of Queen Anne most silver teapots were shaped like gourds or melons. (You will be fortunate indeed if you can buy a genuine silver teapot made before 1714 for a sum that will not rock you back pretty smartly on your heels.) Many silver teapots made after 1765 were octagonal in shape, and often were richly decorated with flowers, garlands or stylised ornamentation. Later still the leading silversmiths were influenced successively by Thomas Sheraton (that is, about the year 1776) and by George Hepplewhite (*circa* 1789). The discoveries made at Pompeii and Herculaneum during the reign of George III had a significant effect, too, on the

A graceful silver teapot, on a stand, made by Peter and Anne Bateman, of London, at the end of the eighteenth century.

silversmiths of the time, and many silver teapots made during the last decades of the eighteenth century were designed—to appeal to the tastes of the fashionable world— in Greek and Roman styles.

While it would be quite misleading to pretend that there are many unrecognised eighteenth-century silver teapots about, ready to be picked up for very small sums, it has to be recorded that occasionally a treasure does turn up unexpectedly, to make a pleasant surprise for some fortunate owner. One silver teapot appeared recently as a contribution to the campaign organised to prevent London's third airport being sited in the farmland of Hertfordshire.

The teapot was one of the lots in an auction sale held at Barkway Village Hall in aid of the Nuthampstead Preservation Association. It was given to the organisers by a woman who observed briefly, 'This thing is supposed to be silver.'

Silver? The 'thing' turned out to be a fine example of the work of the Georgian silversmith Hester Bateman. It was made in 1783 and engraved with the crest of the Black Douglas family. A very similar teapot on show at that time at the Antique Dealers' Fair at Grosvenor House in London was priced at £2,400.

In the years 1800–5 the first silver tea services were created. (By the words 'tea service', people in the trade mean a matching set of tea-table pieces, which will probably comprise a teapot, a hot water jug, a cream jug and a sugar basin.) As the Victorian age brought increasing prosperity to the upper and middle classes of England, and as 'afternoon tea' became more and more widely accepted as a social occasion, and as an opportunity for entertaining (and for 'showing off' a family's status symbols) the silver tea service—big, weighty and covered with too much fussy decoration—became one of the most important features in the furnishings of the home. Today we tend to find these later nineteenth-century domestic treasures much too florid and cumbersome for our taste. (Those that have survived, that is. Having a considerable melt-down value, and not much aesthetic appeal, more of these have vanished than remain to add an unmistakable flavour of pre-Raphaelite splendour to our collections of silver.) Come by through gift or inheritance, they are by no means to be despised. The pendulum of taste swings slowly, but it swings inevitably. Who knows?—By the time our great-grandchildren are starting their collections of silver the few Victorian tea services that remain by that time may be valued as highly as the best Georgian silver coffee pots are rated today.

CHAPTER TWELVE

SILVER TEA-KETTLES

Most silver teapots made during the eighteenth century were quite small, and needed to be refilled rather frequently. It was usual, then, to have a matching tea-kettle as part of the tea-table equipage. This tea-kettle would normally be made to a shape (octagonal, possibly, or round) which was not markedly different from that of the teapot it was intended to supply. Unlike the teapot, it would have a hinged handle (provided, usually, with a grip made of ebony or some other material that does not conduct heat very easily). And it would have a small lamp beneath it to keep the water it contained as hot as possible for as long as possible. Normally, this lamp would be fitted in a tripod stand, or a stand with four legs.

Genuine and undamaged silver tea-kettles that date from the eighteenth century now change hands for very high prices, so there are many other examples of the silversmith's craft to which the average collector will give a higher priority on his or her shopping list.

CHAPTER THIRTEEN

COLLECTING TEA CADDIES

Tea leaves, we have shown, were once almost prohibitively expensive. Any consumable material that is as valuable as this is liable to dwindle away where there are servants who are not scrupulously honest. So silversmiths worked hard during the early part of the eighteenth century to produce special containers or 'caddies' in which the desirable leaves could be kept safely under lock and key. Genuine examples of these early caddies tend to be very expensive, but they are almost invariably graceful and attractive, and even if one cannot afford the pleasures of ownership one can get a lot of satisfaction from looking out for, and studying, the examples on view in the great public collections, such as that in the Victoria and Albert Museum.

To picture them correctly in their true domestic setting one has to imagine most of the early silver tea caddies as they would normally have been accommodated—in thief-proof cases made of some especially attractive wood such as rosewood or satinwood, or, sometimes, made of a commoner wood covered with shagreen. In most cases these outer containers would be given a little extra quality with silver embellishments. A pair of caddies would normally be housed, in the early days, in each case.

In the later days of the eighteenth century tea caddies were often made up in sets of three—a large caddy, intended to contain tea from China (which had then, as now, relatively large leaves) and two less commodious caddies, meant for the smaller leaves of green and black or 'bohea' tea. (Frequently the lady of the house would enjoy blending the leaves to suit her own personal taste.)

When tea became so cheap—relatively speaking—that it was not so much worth stealing, and there was no longer so much necessity for the silver caddies to be locked away for

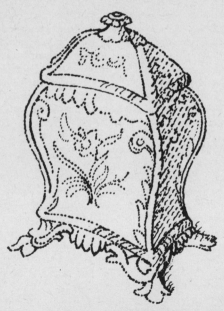

A silver tea caddy made in 1762.

the sake of their contents, silversmiths were able to depart from the conventional square and round forms and, instead, to experiment with oval, octagonal and other less predictable shapes.

By the middle of the eighteenth century round-shouldered caddies and caddies shaped like vases were being produced in relatively large numbers, and the bulbous form known as *bombé* was also very popular. Tea caddies of this period were rarely plain—rather, every suitable surface would be chased with floral decorations, 'Rococo' embellishments or armorial bearings. The oriental origins of tea, too, stimulated the development of 'chinoiserie' decorations—Chinese figures and scenes of Chinese life being frequently found.

Tea caddies that date from the reign of George IV can be bought for much smaller sums than coffee-pots of the same period, and a Victorian caddy should be within the reach of any serious collector.

CHAPTER FOURTEEN

COLLECTING CREAM JUGS

In the earliest days of tea-drinking it was not usual to add milk or sugar to the newly introduced beverage. By the reign of Queen Anne, though, it was becoming usual for the strong taste of the green leaves to be made slightly more palatable (for those who found the flavour a little over-powering) by the discreet introduction of cream. The new fashion was considered to be distinctly vulgar by those of the highest class. 'I must further advise you, Harriet,' says a society lady to her daughter in a play *The Fool of Quality* published a little later in the century, 'not to heap such mountains of sugar into your tea, nor to pour such a deluge of cream in; people will certainly take you for the daughter of a dairymaid. There is young Fanny Quirp, who is a lady by birth, and she has brought herself to the perfection of never suffering the tincture of her tea to be spoiled by whitening, nor the flavour to be adulterated by a grain of sweet.'

In spite of this lofty condemnation, the cream jug quickly became a necessary part of the furnishings of all but the most dignified tea-tables, and silversmiths were hard put to it to satisfy the sudden demand. Today, a silver cream jug from an earlier century is a treasured possession in a great many homes. Though it is possible to find many admirable examples for sale through the trade, the prices usually asked for these tend to take the cream jug out of the range of the 'first pieces of silver to collect'.

The earliest cream jugs—those made during the reign of Queen Anne, that is—were mostly very plain and made chiefly for utility (in form, many of them resembled the jugs that had been in use for beer). Then the helmet-shaped jug was developed, by both London and Irish silversmiths (the shape of one of these jugs is roughly that of a helmet inverted, not as it would have set on a man's head). Many of the London jugs stood on moulded bases, the Irish silversmiths generally preferring to make jugs that stood on three legs.

An eighteenth-century silver cream jug of Irish origin.

Before long, cream jugs were being produced in a wide variety of styles—those shaped like ewers being especially popular. As the eighteenth century wore on, much chasing and elaborate repoussé work was added to these jugs to provide extra interest to what is, after all, a comparatively simple form. (At the height of the Rococo movement it seemed improper to leave a single surface undecorated.)

Towards the end of the eighteenth century the rage for all things classical started to affect even the production of cream jugs. By the end of the century jugs shaped like classical vases and classical urns had largely replaced the jugs with 'baluster' and bulbous forms that had been so popular earlier. Some extremely elegant jugs can be found which have their feet standing on square bases or plinths like the vases found at Pompeii and Herculaneum.

A 'cow creamer' jug made by John Schuppe. The removable lid, made in the form of a saddle, is bordered with flowers, and has a bee to act as a handle.

Many lovers of eighteenth-century silver like to have at least one 'cow creamer' in their collections. These were small cream jugs made to resemble portly, well-fed cows, the cream being introduced into the cow's body through a hinged lid placed where the saddle should be, and being poured out through the cow's mouth, which formed a spout. The originator of these amusing and attractive little pieces is believed to have been a London silversmith named John Schuppe, who soon found his wares in great demand. Other silversmiths followed his example, introducing slight variations in the form and decoration of their bovine models. Unfortunately this is one of the spheres of silverwork where the 'reproducer' has been especially active, and a collector offered what appears to be an eighteenth-century example should be as careful as he or she can be to ensure that it is genuine.

CHAPTER FIFTEEN

COLLECTING SILVER SUGAR TONGS

When it first became socially acceptable for sugar to be taken in tea, one could not go round to the supermarket to buy a 'pound of granulated' or a 'packet of lump' as one can today. In those days sugar was purchased in the form of hard loaf, and pieces had to be chipped or smashed off this before they could be taken to the tea table in the family's elegant silver sugar bowls. It was considered rude then, as now, for fingers to be used for transferring the sugar from the bowl to the teacup. As aids to polite living, then, the silversmiths of the middle decades of the eighteenth century started to produce elongated tongs that were operated on the same principle as a pair of scissors—when one pressed the handle ends together, the arms, shaped so that they could grip, came together to get a firm purchase on the selected piece of sugar loaf.

The introduction of the sugar tongs coincided with the spread of a certain air of playfulness in the best silversmithing circles, and tongs were promptly produced in a wide range of weird and wonderful shapes. Sometimes a pair of tongs would be fashioned so that it resembled a bird with a very long beak, the bird's feet being used as finger holds, the tips of the bird's bill being used to grip the sugar. In other instances, the tongs might be designed to represent some human being of a particularly fanciful kind such as a clown or a mandarin. Tongs in the form of animals, too, are occasionally found.

Collectors of silver fall generally into one of two principal categories: (*a*) those who like to acquire one or two choice examples only of every kind of article made in silver that can be usefully employed in the home; and (*b*) those who prefer to specialise, limiting their interest to pieces of one particular type and collecting as many variations as possible within their chosen field. For collectors of the second type, eighteenth-century sugar tongs provide an unusually rewarding opportunity. They are sufficiently plentiful to be valued well below the 'millionaires only' price-tag bracket without being so lacking in character that they can ever seem commonplace.

Towards the end of the eighteenth century the 'scissors' form of the sugar tongs was generally abandoned, and the form more usually found today—shaped, if looked at sideways, like a letter U with elongated uprights—became fashionable. Tongs of this, the newer, kind offered inventive silversmiths almost as much opportunity for playful enterprise as the tongs of the outmoded scissors type. The ends that were to grip the pieces of sugar became (before they left the workbenches of the more frivolous craftsmen) hands, claws, talons, leaves, seashells and other more fanciful natural objects.

You have already read the section that deals with the hall-marks that have been stamped on approved silver articles through the centuries. Don't look for hall-marks too resolutely if you decide to collect early sugar tongs. Sugar tongs fall into one of the few categories that have been designated from time to time as 'exempted articles'.

If hall-marks are to be seen on them at all, it will probably be because the silversmith concerned was an exceptionally careful businessman, or unusually pleased with his work.

CHAPTER SIXTEEN

COLLECTING SILVER 'BASKETS' MADE FOR BREAD, CAKE AND FRUIT

As the silversmiths of the eighteenth century became more readily able to manipulate sheet silver in what we, today, might call a 'light fantastic way', they turned their talents profitably to the production of 'baskets' for bread, cake and fruit that were to rival most effectively the splendid porcelain dishes we also associate with the last decades of that century. Many of these baskets were magnificently chased and contained pierced work of very high quality. After the middle of the century most of the baskets were fitted with 'swing' handles that were, themselves, pierced with decorative designs so effectively that they seem to be practically without weight. A genuine eighteenth-century silver basket is liable, if it is undamaged, to cost a lot of money. If it comes from the workshop of a really famous silversmith such as Paul de Lamerie (died 1751) it may well set the lucky purchaser back a small fortune.

There are, however, many silver bread, cake and fruit baskets made in the nineteenth century that hardly fall in the 'luxury goods' category at all. These may not have individually designed pierced work, like that found on the earlier, dearly prized baskets. They may even be machine made. It is more than possible (if they have been made at a fairly late date in the century) that they will be made of 'silver plate', rather than silver. But, even with these qualifications, they may well be worth acquiring, for they will probably look noticeably more attractive in a contemporary setting than many of the comparable articles of table furniture made and marketed today.

CHAPTER SEVENTEEN

COLLECTING SILVER LADLES AND OTHER EATING AND DRINKING ACCESSORIES

Silver ladles used for serving punch and other hot drinks are popular with collectors, and so are the later, and more numerous, ladles used for serving soup. Often ladles dating from the late eighteenth or early nineteenth centuries will be found in sets. A set may consist of a ladle for punch with one or more ladles for soup, or occasionally of a ladle or two with various kinds of spoons.

Silver sauce ladles that date from the Georgian and Regency periods are still to be found at prices that make them really accessible. Other table accessories from these eras, such as the silver scoops used for extracting the marrow from meat bones, may be encountered occasionally. The difficulty, with these outmoded pieces, is to recognise them for what they are—or were!

Victorian silversmiths and manufacturers of silver goods were endlessly inventive in their search for new 'lines' that would prove popular. Silver and electro-plated spoons with richly embossed bowls were made for serving the various jams, jellies and moulds under which the tables of the more fortunate Victorians groaned; special forks were designed for spearing fruit, pickles, sardines and many other eatables; scissor-like tongs were devised for gripping grapes; crackers in an almost endless range of fantastic shapes were produced for removing the kernels from nuts; and many more table accessories were made and marketed that are only a little less frequently encountered than these. This is, in fact, a very rewarding field to explore for anyone starting to collect silver.

CHAPTER EIGHTEEN

COLLECTING SILVER DRINKING VESSELS

Nowadays the words 'silver drinking vessel' will probably mean, to the uninitiated, merely the round silver tankards that are given as coming-of-age presents, or are kept for favoured customers to drink their beer from in the more handsomely appointed public houses. But there is much more to the subject than this. Anyone who starts to collect silver seriously will soon encounter a number of puzzling terms:

Mazers were not made after the time of Queen Elizabeth I, and they are only mentioned here because examples may be seen in public collections or referred to in books. They were round bowls—made usually of maple wood, and decorated with silver bands, silver rims and other mountings. Definitely for millionaires only.

Flagons were made in the days of the late Tudors—fine heavy ones, too, broader at the base than at the neck, so that they were less prone to be knocked over. They were often chased and embossed with flowers and formal patterns, and were completed with hinged covers.

Porringers and Posset pots. After Charles II returned from exile to a country that had been denuded by a long Civil War of much of its best silver plate, he was to preside over a quarter of a century of frantic refurnishing. Most of his subjects who had any money at all preferred to invest in a large number of comparatively small pieces of silver plate, that would be generally useful in the day-to-day life of their households, rather than in one or two very grand pieces, the principal function of which would be show. Among the small silver objects that were produced in great quantities at

The shape of an early porringer.

this time was the 'porringer'. This was an open cup of moderate size with sides that were almost parallel and a lip that turned slightly outwards. There were two handles, at opposite sides of the cup, that helped to give the whole vessel a delightfully well-balanced and symmetrical shape. The posset pot was very similar to the porringer, but it was fitted with a cover—possibly, some experts have suggested, to give some protection against the poisoner. You may remember Lady Macbeth's hospitable words:

> *I have drugged their possets,*
> *That death and nature do contend about them,*
> *Whether they live or die . . .*

Porringers and posset pots were used principally for serving hot strong drinks, most often as 'nightcaps'. The word 'posset' may have been applied to a hot spiced wine, or to a thicker beverage, made with sack, spices, eggs and milk. 'Caudle', too (hot curdled milk, made more appetising with wine and hot spices) would be taken from these little vessels. There is an obvious connection between the words 'porringer' and 'porridge' and it is possible that sometimes they would be used for serving gruel.

Tankards were developed logically from the flagon, and came into use fairly generally during the seventeenth century. A tankard of that period will normally be round, and again, a little broader at the base than at the neck. It will have a hinged cover, which will probably be flat, or nearly so. It will certainly be very expensive—out of reach of all but the wealthiest collectors.

During the eighteenth century, silver tankards continued to be made in very much the same form as they had been for the previous hundred years. Some silversmiths, though, made instead cylindrical tankards with sides that did not taper either way, and others made tankards that were curved or bulbous. Tankards of all these kinds were frequently decorated with chased ornament or engraved heraldic designs, and lids were generally fitted. (You will be lucky if you find an eighteenth-century tankard in any bargain basement: they are inevitably highly valued.)

The biggest change in the history of the tankard came during the first decades of the nineteenth century, when tankards without lids became popular. Victorian cylindrical tankards and tankards that are straight-sided but narrower at the top than the bottom have been collected eagerly in recent years, and prices are high. On the whole, silver tank-

An early silver tankard.

ards (other than modern ones) are not the most promising field for anyone trying to start a collection.

Beakers. Again, one is only likely to come across in a museum or in one of the great internationally known collections, a genuine silver or silver gilt beaker made in the reign of one of the Stuart kings. These tall, elegant drinking vessels, the sides of which turn out slightly as they near the rim, were the precursors of the modern drinking glass. Fine examples are worth studying, wherever they can be seen, even if there is little chance of them passing into your private hands. Plain beakers, made during the nineteenth century, come up occasionally.

Wine Cups. The silver wine cups of the seventeenth century were, again, the predecessors of the glass vessels from which wine is most often taken today. Genuine examples that date from before the Civil War are few, genuine examples made in the decades that immediately followed the Restoration are more numerous, but on the rare occasions on which they change hands, do so for large sums. But for the ordinary collector without unlimited private means there *are* silver wine vessels to be picked up at moderately reasonable prices—there was a revival of interest in pieces of this kind during the nineteenth century, and late Victorian wine cups, resembling domestic egg cups, enhanced by considerable areas of delicate engraving, can be found in silver or in electro-plate, in many antique shops and shops that sell general bric-à-brac, and may be well worth purchasing even if, through neglect, they are now a little tarnished.

CHAPTER NINETEEN

'MONTEITHS'

It is difficult for anyone living today in a centrally heated home to appreciate how uncomfortable winters' nights could be in, say, the seventeenth century. In the chill, draughty mansions of those days, leaving a glowing fireplace and going away to bed through long unheated passages must have been an unpleasant business. So the consumption of strong warming drinks at bedtime became more than a habit, it was almost a necessity. The capacious silver vessels in which these drinks were served are valued as highly today by collectors as they were then by the people who derived comfort from their contents.

A 'Monteith' is a special kind of silver punch bowl. It has a notched or scalloped rim that is sometimes removable and sometimes an integral part of the bowl. Wine glasses could be suspended bowl downwards in a Monteith, the feet or bases of the glasses being held securely by the raised portions of the rim. No one knows for certain how the Monteith got its name. One colourful theory is that it was called after its inventor, a Scotsman known as 'Monteith' or 'Monteigh' who is said to have worn a cloak with a scalloped edge. Most of the Monteiths that have been satisfactorily located are now in museums or in valuable collections.

CHAPTER TWENTY

COLLECTING SILVER WINE TASTERS

These are little dishes that are not unlike porringers, but are much shallower. (Some may even be only an inch and a half deep, so that they resemble saucers, rather than drinking vessels.) They were used, as their name implies, for sampling the wines imported into this country under conditions that were much less strictly managed than those that pertain today. Being so shallow, they allowed a possible purchaser to study closely the colour of the wine that was poured into them. Some were even made with raised centres as the bottom of a wine bottle is commonly made today.

Having been so rarely written up, wine tasters are liable to be passed over unrecognised when the contents of homes

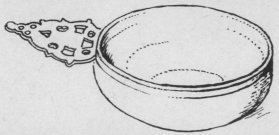

A silver 'bleeding bowl' of the kind used by surgeons in the late eighteenth and early nineteenth centuries.

are disposed of. Occasionally they may even be confused with the silver 'bleeding bowls' that were part of the standard therapeutic equipment of surgeons in the late seventeenth and early eighteenth centuries. (Marks inside the bowls of these were intended to show when the patient had been relieved of enough of the troubling fluid.) It is the keen-eyed collector who keeps looking for these little vessels that goes happily home with the gravy.

CHAPTER TWENTY-ONE

COLLECTING SILVER WINE AND
SPIRIT LABELS

During the eighteenth century and the greater part of the
nineteenth, it was customary to serve wines and spirits from
elegant white flint glass decanters instead of (as so often
today) by pouring them straight from the bottle. It was a
civilised way of treating wines that tended to throw sedi-
ments, but it imposed one small obligation on the owners, or
the keepers, of the decanters—these had to be labelled in
some way so that their contents could be readily identified.

At first it seemed sufficient for a decanter to have the
name of some wine or spirit permanently incorporated in its
outer surface, and very charmingly many of these early
decanters were inscribed. Then it was realised that a decanter so marked could only be properly used for one particular kind of fluid, and that an economy would be achieved
if its contents could be varied. Down in the dark recesses of
gentlemen's cellars there were in use, already, some relatively crude labels—made, usually, of pottery—that served
for marking the different bins. The decanters used on the
table obviously needed some more refined labelling. So
small elegant name-plaques were produced in gold,
porcelain, Battersea and other enamels, and—of particular interest to the reader of this book—in silver. These

were usually fitted with chains or wires that enabled them to be hung without any difficulty over the decanter's neck. Occasionally, a wine label may be found in the form of a ring.

Silver wine labels as decorative as this can still be collected for relatively small sums.

There are already many keen collectors of silver wine labels (there is, even, a Wine Label Circle, to which many enthusiasts belong). But, there are still plenty of opportunities for those who have not yet started to collect. More than five hundred different kinds of label have been recorded, the spellings on some of them—'Champaigne', 'Champaign' and 'Champagne', for example, showing a remarkable degree of variation. Some of the wines shown, too, such as 'Tent' and 'Paraketta' are quite unfamiliar today. Occasionally, a label may turn up with an amusing legend, such as 'Nig' instead of 'Gin'. Some of the greatest silversmiths have produced these decorative little labels. If you would like to have in your collection a genuine example of the work of, say, Hester Bateman or Paul Storr, examine carefully every silver wine label you come across. There are surprises marked on the back of some of them, as well as on the fronts!

CHAPTER TWENTY-TWO

SILVER WINE COOLERS

It would be unrealistic to head this section 'Collecting Silver Wine Coolers', because these vessels, to serve their intended purpose adequately, had to be very large and heavy, and those made by the most reputable silversmiths tend to be extremely expensive. However, one is liable to come across some magnificent specimens (invariably, very richly adorned) in the representative public collections, so anyone acquiring a knowledge of silver should at least know what these pieces are.

Most of the silver wine coolers maade in the eighteenth and early nineteenth centuries were designed to suggest, without any possibility of a mistake being made, the wealth and importance of their owners. Each had facilities for the storage of ice—usually in a removable container. In the second half of the nineteenth century some wine coolers were made in the newly invented 'Electro-plate' (see an account of this, later in this book). These coolers, and these coolers only, change hands at prices that the average person can hope to afford.

CHAPTER TWENTY-THREE

COLLECTING SALT CELLARS

Valuable and interesting collections could be made of silver salt cellars alone, so varied and beautiful have been these almost indispensable articles of tableware produced by British silversmiths during the past four or five centuries.

The earliest salt cellars we know about were used to divide those taking meat together into separate social classes—those sitting 'above the salt' being thought worthy of honour, those sitting below it being lumped together unceremoniously as 'the rest'. Most of the grand 'standing salts' of the Tudor and Stuart eras are now treasured in the great internationally famous collections, such as that belonging to the Worshipful Company of Goldsmiths, in London, or are owned by one of the more careful Corporations (the Corporation of Norwich, for example, has a splendid silver gilt salt and cover that was made in that city as early as 1568), or appear on ceremonial occasions on the tables of the more fortunate colleges of the more venerable universities. Only one of the wealthiest oil or shipping magnates would be likely to afford easily, say, a condiment container of the quality of the Gibbon Salt, made in 1576 and presented to the Goldsmiths on Saint Bartholomew's Day 1632 by Simon Gibbon, if any masterpiece as valuable as that should appear again on the open market. Even as early as 1903 a $11\frac{3}{8}$-inch high-standing salt of the time of

James I, with the London mark for 1613 was sold at Christie's salerooms for £1,150, and we all know what kind of money that would be in today's terms.

But there is no reason why those of us with more modest means should not take our salt from examples of the silver-smith's craft that are just as useful and considerably less ornate. The cellars made in Queen Anne's days and during the Georgian period are of unexcelled elegance, and change hands at considerably less astronomical sums.

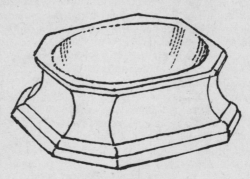

A silver salt cellar of the 'trencher' type.

Take, for instance, the 'trencher' salt. In the days of the Tudors and Stuarts, the trencher type of salt cellar was provided only for the humble feeders at the less exalted end of a communal dining-table—the gentry, for whom a stand-ing salt would be provided, having no need or wish to dip the ends of their knives in what was little more than a menial trough. As time went on, however, and manners changed, trencher salts came into more general use, and by the beginning of the eighteenth century were being produced in some quantities. During the first quarter of that century the form of the trencher salt did not change much—it was usually oblong or octagonal—but during the reign of George II 'legged' cellars appeared which were, in effect, trencher salts that had been raised slightly off the surface of the table. Suddenly, as if this was a signal that released them from certain traditional inhibitions, the silversmiths of the period became furiously inventive in the salt-cellar field.

It will be impossible to give here a comprehensive list of the different kinds of silver salt cellar that were produced during the rest of the eighteenth century and the nineteenth century because these are too numerous to be catalogued in a short introductory guide of this sort. However, among those particularly worth looking out for are the following:

The *circular salt cellar*, raised, usually, on three feet, that dates from the first decades of George III's long reign, and has been made ever since in various forms.

The *salt cellar made from pierced sheet*. Usually, a cellar of this kind would be raised on four feet, each of which would be made to resemble a lion's paw, or to the well-

A circular silver salt cellar of a type that has kept its popularity for many decades.

known 'ball and claw' design. It would probably be oval or oblong in shape, and it would have a specially made glass lining (normally blue) to contain the salt.

The *boat-shaped salt cellar*, which dates from the end of the eighteenth century. Often a cellar of this kind will have a long, gracefully curved handle.

In the Victorian era, silver salt cellars were produced in a great variety of styles and designs, many of these being so florid and ornate that they appeal only to those with a taste for the unusual and exotic. Before you invest too rashly in a nineteenth-century salt 'cell' (as the cellar came to be called at that time) there are three points to consider carefully— will it do the job for which it is intended? (some were designed without a thought being given to their primary function); can it be kept clean and hygienic? (many were so heavily loaded with ornament and so deeply fretted that they could hardly fail to collect and harbour foreign matter); and, have you the kind of cutlery that will sit with it agreeably?

CHAPTER TWENTY-FOUR

COLLECTING SILVER SAUCE-BOATS

A dining-table of the mid-eighteenth century must have been a fine sight when set out with all a family's newly acquired silverware. Occupying a fairly prominent place would inevitably be one or more silver sauce-boats.

The earliest sauce-boats known to have been used in this country (late in the seventeenth century) had oval-shaped bodies. Each had a lip, for pouring, in the centre of each side, and handles at both ends. After 1730 the 'boat'-shaped vessel became fashionable—in this type, which we still know so well today, there is just one pouring lip, at one end, and a single handle at the other. The handles were often made playfully to resemble heraldic animals, 'caryatids' (human figures) or dragons. The earlier sauce-boats were usually set firmly on moulded bases. Later sauce-boats were made to stand on three or four short legs, terminating in feet that were often made to resemble lions' paws, sea-shells or other decorative features.

The collector looking for silver sauce-boats today has still many opportunities to pick up some fine specimens, since these handsome little vessels have remained constantly in favour—and in constant production—for such a long period of time.

CHAPTER TWENTY-FIVE

COLLECTING SILVER SALVERS

Actually, 'Collecting Silver Salvers' may be an over-ambitious heading for this section of this book. In most homes a single silver salver will be sufficient for everyday use—with, perhaps, a second example if resources will stretch to it. But most eighteenth- and early nineteenth-century salvers are so attractive and so much sought after that they are rarely undervalued.

During the Stuart period the piece we now know as a 'salver' would usually be made with a cup or tankard in matching style, and it would probably be used as a small tray on which the drinking vessel could be carried around. In the early eighteenth century the salver was usually called a 'table'. At this time it usually took the form of a large heavy dish—sometimes standing on a central foot—and it would normally be used merely as an impressive piece of sideboard plate.

Some of the finest salvers that have survived from this period came into existence as a result of an interesting old custom. Since the sixteenth century it had been usual for the Officer of State responsible for the Great Seal or any other seal of office to be given the silver matrix as his special perquisite when the seal became outdated on the death of the Sovereign, or on a change in his title. From this matrix, melted down, a salver would be made, and it would be engraved with a representation of the obsolete seal.

To most silver collectors, though, the word 'salver' will mean something considerably less grand and ostentatious than this. Many of those made early in the eighteenth century were relatively simple, with moulded edges. Later, salvers with gadrooned (that is, 'pie crust') edges became popular. A large proportion of the salvers made during the eighteenth and early nineteenth centuries were engraved—at some point in their existence—with the armorial bearings of their owners. Carried out by a skilful craftsman, this form of decoration can add considerably to the appearance of a salver and (if it has been done at the time the salver was made) may even enhance its interest and value.

Certain silversmiths seem to have specialised, during the late eighteenth century, in making silver trays. (A silver tray can be regarded without too much inaccuracy as a large salver, though it will probably be oval or oblong, rather than round, and it will almost certainly have two graceful handles, usually decorated with silver 'foliage'.) Many of these trays are very large—some of them measure more than 3 feet between the handles—and they are proportionately heavy. With their elegant borders and finely designed engraved decoration these trays are among the most useful and admirable examples of the silversmith's craft to have survived from that splendid century.

CHAPTER TWENTY-SIX

COLLECTING SILVER CASTERS

Silver casters, from which sugar, spice and dry mustard could be sprinkled, became part of the well-to-do householder's table furniture at the end of the seventeenth century and have remained so, without any break, right up to the present day. Early casters tend to be expensive, late Victorian examples can still be picked up for smaller sums. As these are likely to be most decorative adjuncts to any domestic display of china and glass they are generally an excellent investment.

The earliest casters were invariably small, and were mostly cylindrical in form and fairly plain. Early in the eighteenth century, however, silversmiths started to experiment with a number of other shapes, each of which took the fashionable fancy for a time until it was ousted by some new development. Many of these eighteenth-century casters had bulbous or 'baluster' bodies encircled by a distinctive band. Above this band the body would be relatively slender, and would usually terminate in a beautifully pierced dome or 'cover', surmounted by a baluster knob. At various times during the eighteenth century this knob would be given a shape that made it quite different from knobs of an earlier period—casters made in the reign of George II, for example, frequently having knobs made to resemble pine cones. Occasionally, examples are found that are quite richly

A silver caster, with attractive pierced work, made in London in the 1760s.

decorated with chased or repoussé embellishments (flowers and rococo ribands being among the favourite motifs of the silversmiths and their patrons) but, more often, the casters of the period were expected to rely for their effect on the general elegance of their form, with the richness of their pierced covers as an additional attraction.

CHAPTER TWENTY-SEVEN

COLLECTING SILVER CANDLESTICKS

It is difficult for us to imagine today what life must have been like before electric power became generally available in the home. We take so much for granted the advantages of instant touch-a-switch lighting and heating. In most households candles are only kept for rare emergencies—if, in fact, they are bothered with at all. It is salutary to remember that only a century ago candlesticks were among the most important items in the equipment of the ordinary home. Many of these—made purely for utility—were cheap products of the pottery industry, or were turned out in brass, copper or Sheffield plate. Enough were made in silver, by expert craftsmen, both in London and the Provinces, for the addition of two or three admirable examples to a collection to be a perfectly reasonable proposition.

The earliest candlesticks of which we have any accurate record were those made for church use. These are usually referred to as 'pricket' candlesticks, since each would have a strong spike on which the candle could be securely impaled. (The sight of a heavy candle heeling over sideways at the climax of a solemn religious service was liable to be a little disconcerting.)

No genuine candlesticks made before Charles II's reign are likely to come the way of the private collector who is not a millionaire or is not inheriting the possessions of a millionaire. Being, in view of the function they have to perform, fairly heavy objects, all too few survived the great melting-down campaigns of the Civil War.

After the return of Charles II from exile, replacements were produced as rapidly as possible. Influenced by the rather florid styles of dress and furniture that became fashionable towards the end of that century, silversmiths tended to favour candlesticks with stems modelled boldly to resemble human figures or animals. Not many of these have survived, as they were bulky and heavy, and when the style ceased to be fashionable they were (once again) melted down for the sake of the metal they contained.

The eighteenth century was the great age of candle-light, and the salons of the wealthy and elegant were, for the most part, brilliantly lit. Silver table candlesticks were made during the century in a wide variety of designs. Most large houses contained literally dozens of pairs, and in consequence the candlestick is almost the commonest surviving article of English silver plate of that century. Even in the later years of the nineteenth century, when more convenient and efficient methods of lighting were being introduced into cities and towns, those in the remoter rural areas continued to depend on lamplight and candle-light.

The designs from which the collector can choose are numerous. All eighteenth- and early nineteenth-century candlesticks have, as a necessary feature, a broad base, which may be circular, oval or square. From this may rise a stem that swells most elegantly in what is usually known as 'baluster' fashion. Each silversmith who made candlesticks had his own favourite methods of decorating them—with fluting, possibly, or with beaded ornament. During the Rococo period, a profusion of scrolls and foliage appeared on candlesticks that were otherwise quite simply designed,

93

but many collectors today prefer the austere elegance of the 'classical' candlesticks produced under the influence of the great architects and decorators Robert and Charles Adam.

A 'branched' silver candlestick is often referred to as a 'candelabrum'. This is an elegant, though comparatively simple, example.

'Branched' silver candlesticks—those which have two, three or more arms, to carry a number of candles—were popular throughout the eighteenth and early nineteenth centuries and may make a fine show, today, on a dining-table or on a polished wood sideboard. When purchasing any silver candlesticks produced after the middle of the eighteenth century it is advisable to remember that it became quite a common practice, then, for silversmiths to add extra weight

94

to a hollow candlestick by filling its interior with resin. Other silversmiths preferred to work with some cheaper metal, casing it only in silver. These expedients may make no real difference to the outward appearance of a 'silver' candlestick, but they do mean, of course, that its total weight is not that of the silver it contains.

During the long reign of Queen Victoria, silver candlesticks—and other pieces—were often produced especially for presentation to notable people as public testimonials, or to be shown in exhibitions. The London firm of Hunt and Roskell is particularly remembered for ornate pieces of this kind that were designed to display 'the application of silver to sculpture and decoration'. These showpieces lacked, needless to say, the elegant simplicity of the best work made during the Regency Period. Typical of this extravagantly naturalistic work that most collectors today would appreciate merely for its curiosity value were two candlesticks, made as part of a testimonial to the Earl of Ellenborough to commemorate his achievements in India. When these candlesticks were shown at the Great Exhibition of 1851, this is how they were listed in the official catalogue:

Two candelabra. Stems and branches composed of a vine on a base of Indian architecture. Figures of a British grenadier, European officer of native infantry, foot-artillery soldier, horse-artillery man, native light-cavalry trooper, and a trooper of the irregular horse. The bases are supported by recumbent camels . . .

At the same exhibition the firm of T. Wilkinson and Company showed a candelabrum made to resemble a date palm under which there sheltered the two figures of 'Paul et Virginie'. Garrards', eventually, were awarded the

Goldsmiths' Company's prize for the best piece of plate shown at the Exhibition—they won it with a candelabrum-centrepiece 'in the Moorish style' that depicted a scene from Sir Walter Scott's novel *The Talisman*. From this distance of time we can only say, 'Those were the days!'

CHAPTER TWENTY-EIGHT

COLLECTING SILVER SNUFFERS

Snuffers were used in the days when candles had to be trimmed frequently if they were to give a satisfactory light. The need for these little domestic appliances continued through an extended period of English history, for wicks that burned slowly, giving a steady and stable flame, were not introduced into candle-making until quite late in the nineteenth century.

The earliest snuffers were rather like scissors or shears, each pair having one blade specially formed to take off the redundant wick when the candle was snuffed. Usually, these snuffers were quite rudimentary, and made of iron. Later snuffers usually incorporated a small box in which the smouldering wick was caught without having to be dealt with by the fingers. In some snuffers, this box was made up of two parts, one fitted to each blade, that combined to form a whole when the blades met. Improved versions, brought in later still, had a box attached to one blade only, the other blade being fitted with a flat plate that pressed the smouldering wick, immediately after it had been cut off, against the inside of the box, extinguishing it, and minimising what must have been an extremely objectionable smell.

Silver candle snuffers produced in the eighteenth and early nineteenth centuries were frequently very ornate. Seeing no reason for the snuffer boxes to be purely functional and rectangular, fashion-conscious silversmiths produced them in circular, oval and even heart shapes, enriching them, like the rest of the snuffer, with much embossed or engraved decoration. Many snuffers were made with trays, in matching style, on which they were intended to rest when they were not in use. (Small feet are usually found on snuffers of this kind. These were intended to act as supports for the resting snuffer. Sometimes a pair of snuffers will be found to be attached to its tray by a fine silver chain.)

After the introduction of the steadily burning candle-wick, snuffers of the scissors or shears type were no longer needed, but an extinguisher of a different kind was some-times produced. This was a cone-shaped cap of silver that was used in conjunction with the ordinary domestic candle-stick again usually being anchored to it by a length of fine chain. To use the cap, one just had to place it over the top of the candle. All snuffers and candle caps will tend to increase in interest as the reason for their existence fades into history.

CHAPTER TWENTY-NINE

COLLECTING SILVER VINAIGRETTES

The word 'vinaigrette' may be a little confusing, for the world has changed considerably since these delicately made little containers were carried by all those who were keeping up with the latest trends. So the term must be immediately defined.

Nowadays, our general standards of cleanliness and hygiene have risen so satisfactorily that it is not normally any longer necessary for anyone entering a crowded assembly such as a State Ball or a fashion parade or a Bridge or Bingo Session to hold a strongly smelling pomander to his or her nose, as Cardinal Wolsey was forced to do when he went out into company. (That fore-doomed dignitary was accustomed to carrying, as he walked among the populace, an orange or *pomme d'ambre* 'whereof the meat was extracted and the rind filled up with a sponge wherein was Vinegar and other Confections against the Pestilent Airs. To the which, he most commonly smelt when he was pestered with many suitors'.) Ladies and gentlemen in the reigns of 'Farmer' George III, his son who acted as Regent, 'Pineapple William', and the virtuous young Queen Victoria carried, instead of hollowed-out oranges, small 'sponge boxes' that contained, as their name implied, little sponges impregnated with aromatic vinegar. These 'sponge boxes' are known now in the trade as 'vinaigrettes'. There is the promised definition.

Anyone who starts to collect silver vinaigrettes (they were made in gold, too, but those lie outside the scope of this book) is on to a relatively uncomplicated field of activity. Few vinaigrettes—to take only one aspect of the matter—can be convincingly shown to have been faked or forged. No counterfeiter would have found the comparatively small returns worth the trouble. Vinaigrettes were fashioned most delicately in the periods of English history when man-hours (and woman-hours and child-hours) did not have to be counted as carefully as they are today. Now the sharp-eyed collector can acquire for a fraction of their probable value, some exquisite examples of work from one of the great ages of human endeavour.

Most vinaigrettes are shaped like small rectangular boxes, though you may come across some made in other shapes (circular and heart-shaped vinaigrettes are occasionally found) and vinaigrettes made to resemble small books and purses are not uncommon. Invariably, they are richly decorated, some of the most interesting having raised 'views' on their outer surfaces, Westminster Abbey, the Houses of Parliament and other notable buildings being frequently represented.

CHAPTER THIRTY

SOME TERMS, DEFINED

Occasionally a silver collector will come across a technical or trade term that proves puzzling. Here are two names that you may encounter, with brief explanations:

Argyles. Sometimes, in a mixed silver sale, you may come across one or more 'argyles'. These are really only gravy pots, designed to keep the gravy warm on the long journeys that cooked food had so often to make, in domestically less well-organised days, between the kitchen and the dining-room. 'Argyles' usually resemble teapots in their outward appearance, but inside they will almost invariably be found to contain a smaller receptacle for containing hot water, or a heated lump of metal. Sometimes an 'argyle's' handle will be covered with a shield of wicker to make it easier to hold.

Épergnes. These are elaborate centre-pieces, dating usually from the 1760s or a little later, and fine examples usually change hands for considerable sums. A typical épergne might include, among its other components, a scrolled base, a number of dishes or baskets, and one or more sets of candle branches.

CHAPTER THIRTY-ONE

COLLECTING SILVER MEAT SKEWERS

A meat skewer is an item of kitchen equipment of which the present-day housewife, accustomed to dealing principally with the smaller joints (or with steaks, chops, cutlets and pre-packed sausages from the nearest supermarket) may not appreciate the importance. In the eighteenth century, when

The attractive handle end of a mid-eighteenth-century silver meat skewer.

huge quarters and sirloins of beef were less remarkable, and needed to be specially secured for the spit or oven, a cook would reach for a skewer with as little hesitation as his (or her) twentieth-century successor reaches for the aluminium cooking foil. Many of these skewers were made purely for utility, and have not been thought worthy of preservation, but others, made from silver by clever silversmiths and intended to add distinction to the appearance of the meat when it was served are collectors' pieces today. Usually these finer examples have circular terminals, but others may be found (like the one illustrated) that are formed in the shape of a shell or some other decorative motif.

CHAPTER THIRTY-TWO

COLLECTING SILVER INKWELLS

The silver inkwell is another domestic utility for which there is no longer (in these days of fountain and ball-point pens) any real need. In spite of this, a keen collector can sometimes find an inkwell, or even a complete writing stand that will make a pleasant decorative feature in a contemporary home, and will provide an interesting reminder of the times when correspondence was by no means a simple affair.

You will be fortunate indeed if you are offered at any reasonable price a complete eighteenth-century silver writing set or 'standish' (this would probably include a base, with a groove or trough in which the pens would rest; a caster, for sprinkling sand over recent writing to dry the ink; and, possibly, a taperstick for holding a small candle for melting wax for seals; as well as an inkwell). Victorian inkwells, however, are still fairly plentiful, and usually take the form of cut glass ink bottles with silver mountings and silver lids. Stands to take one, two or three of these wells were made in a wide variety of materials, ranging from silver to Irish bog oak. Many had pairs of small upright pegs shaped like the trunks of trees, with two or three stunted branches, on which pens could rest when they were not being used.

CHAPTER THIRTY-THREE

COLLECTING SILVER SPORTING TROPHIES

There is a direct connection between the silver wine cup, made by the nineteenth-century silversmith, and the sports trophies that have been competed for by so many thousands of athletes during the past hundred and fifty years and are still being produced and handed out in such great numbers today. Clearly, a silver trophy of a standard kind will mean more to the person who has won it (or to his closest relatives) than to anyone else, but there are possibilities for collecting in this field, especially among the trophies made in the more florid Victorian and Edwardian days.

Many of these trophies were designed to convey some message about the particular activity for which they were a reward—in a rowing trophy, for instance, the silver bowl might be mounted on a stem made of oars, or a trophy awarded for shooting might incorporate a number of rifles. Horse-racing cups are among the most grandiose of all. One wonders, sometimes, how the proud recipients ever got them home.

CHAPTER THIRTY-FOUR

COLLECTING SILVER BUTTONS

'It's not worth a button!' is a phrase still heard occasionally. But buttons are—strangely enough—collected enthusiastically at the present time in various parts of the world. In the United States of America, for instance, there are button collectors' societies that have large numbers of extremely knowledgeable members.

Silver buttons made in the eighteenth and early nineteenth centuries, being small, are often overlooked. Search carefully through the boxes of unwanted oddments that accumulate in every out-of-the-way junk shop, and you will be bound to find some old silver buttons eventually—and the chances are that they will become yours for a shilling or two each, and no more. Buttons once worn in battle by officers in the Duke of Wellington's army, by sailors who served in the great old ships-of-the-line, and by the members and servants of the most venerable hunts, still continue to turn up among all the dross like pennies from heaven. They are there to be picked up by anyone who has the patience to search for them, and the percipience to recognise them, when found, for what they are. A glance through the pages of *Bailey's Hunting Directory* (to name only one work which can help the collector of buttons) will give some idea of what is involved in this specialised but highly rewarding field.

CHAPTER THIRTY-FIVE

SILVER CHATELAINES

During the late eighteenth and nineteenth centuries, great importance was attached to the keys of the household, and who held them. (Do you remember how David Copperfield's mother was humiliated when the malicious Miss Murdstone took over the keys of her store cupboards?) Then a bunch of keys dangling from a housekeeper's waist was an emblem of importance and domestic authority. Hanging near the bunch, if not closely associated with it, there would probably be a 'chatelaine'—a collection of the small implements such as button-hooks, thimbles, tape measures and scissors that might be needed in the day-to-day running of a household. Often these 'chatelaines' would be made from silver and would be beautifully shaped and richly engraved. When they come on the market in a complete state they are usually snapped up eagerly by collectors. The value of the individual components of Victorian silver chatelaines is rising noticeably too.

CHAPTER THIRTY-SIX

COLLECTING SILVER SNUFF BOXES AND TOBACCO BOXES

The snuff boxes produced for sale to the aristocracy and landed gentry during the eighteenth century—set in jewels, delicately engraved and chased, or bearing even in some cases an exquisitely painted miniature—are hardly likely to be of much immediate interest, for financial reasons, to anyone of average means starting to collect silver. Simpler boxes made in the late Georgian, Regency and Victorian periods can still be picked up at fairly reasonable prices, however—many of them with their original function unrecognised.

CHAPTER THIRTY-SEVEN

SILVER SURGICAL INSTRUMENTS

The wise collector always looks closely at any strange silver implement he may come across, the purpose of which is not immediately apparent. There is a remote chance that the unidentified object may be a surgical instrument that has survived from the days before 'stainless steel' instruments became generally available to the members of the medical fraternity. The curiosity value of these professional bygones never diminishes and their market value has started to rise spectacularly.

CHAPTER THIRTY-EIGHT

SHEFFIELD PLATE

In the year 1743 or thereabouts a man named Thomas Boulsover, of Sheffield, made a very important discovery. He found that an ingot of copper (which was a relatively inexpensive metal) could be given a thin coating of silver, and that the silver could be kept permanently in place by the application of heat. (Since silver melts at 954° C., which is a slightly lower temperature than the melting point of copper, the closely associated metals could be successfully withdrawn from the furnace once the silver had started to liquefy, or 'weep'.) More, he found that the silver-coated copper would retain its more valuable outer skin however thinly it was rolled. As the thickness of the copper decreased, so too did that of the silver.

For a few years Boulsover exploited his discovery by producing buttons, pin boxes and other small saleable articles. Then in the 1750s and 1760s the techniques he had discovered were adopted by his rivals, and soon the production of silver-plated copper goods became one of Sheffield's principal industries. Manufacturers in the Birmingham area, never slow to cash in on commercially valuable processes discovered elsewhere, were soon producing 'Sheffield Plate' wares as attractive as those that were bringing so much increased wealth to Yorkshire.

There is a lot of pleasure and interest to be had from

collecting genuine examples of Sheffield Plate. Anyone with a fairly keen eye will be able to see how these homely goods, produced in the early years of the Industrial Revolution, were fabricated. Usually the various parts were rolled out or stamped out by elementary and ponderous machines. (For example, the bases, tubular stems and upper parts of candlesticks might be formed with steel dies, under the influence of a drop hammer. When all the parts were complete they would be assembled with hard or soft solder.) Usually the goods would be produced by a number of craftsmen, each of whom carried out some separate task at which he was especially skilled, such as designing, shaping or burnishing. This was a tidy step from the traditional methods of the classically trained silversmith, who was expected to carry out all the different processes by himself in a thoroughly competent way. And it made silver goods—or those that were *apparently* silver—available to many more householders than had been able to afford them previously.

In one respect Sheffield Plate articles were better fitted to stand up to a normal amount of domestic wear and tear than those made from silver alone. Copper is considerably stronger than silver, and a piece of Sheffield Plate was therefore less likely to be bent or dented than one made by the more traditional methods. There are many quite splendid Sheffield Plate candlesticks—made purely for utility—that can be found and bought today at prices that are only a fraction of those that would be charged for contemporary silver examples.

In another way Sheffield Plate articles were, and are, more liable to deterioration than their silver equivalents. When Sheffield Plate is worked into shapes that are heavily ridged or chased, the outer coating of silver—which may have been, at the outset, little more than a thousandth of an inch thick—will be subjected to considerable strain, and the projections will be liable to suffer from any unusual friction to which they may be exposed. All too soon, the outer skin of silver will be rubbed away, and the warmer tones of the underlying copper will come to the surface, producing the effect known in the antique goods trade as 'bleeding'. A badly 'bled' piece of Sheffield Plate may be virtually value-less, so if you are offered a well-rubbed entrée dish or some other faithful old family treasure that has seen better days, don't dip too deeply into your housekeeping money in a rush to acquire it. (If it is being practically given away, it may be worth having, to give you a chance to study care-fully how it was made.) If you want it for display, a similar piece in better condition will almost certainly come your way before long at a price not very much greater.

Not all the pieces of old Sheffield Plate you will be offered will be genuine—this is a field in which the faker has been fairly busy, and electro-plated articles, posing as the products of the older industry, are not uncommon. Some experts claim that if the outer silver surface of an electro-plated article is breathed on, the layer of condensation that results will disappear more rapidly than it will from Sheffield Plate. Certainly, the 'breath test', used on genuine Sheffield Plate, will help to show up the faint marks that result where abutting pieces of metal have been joined with silver solder. It will show, too, where pieces of solid silver have been set into the surface of the plate ('inlayed', this is usually called in the trade) to allow crests or armorial bear-ings to be engraved to suit some previous owner. Anyone who has studied closely a sufficient number of genuine pieces of Sheffield Plate will recognise certain unmistakable signs that a piece is 'good'. For instance, it will usually be possible for the close observer to see where an edge has been turned over, like the hem of a sheet, or where a length of silver wire has been soldered on to conceal the exposed copper.

CHAPTER THIRTY-NINE

ELECTRO-PLATE

The art of working in metals was carried on exclusively by the aid of fire until the year 1839. At that epoch, a new light dawned upon the subject; considerable interest was excited in the scientific world, and much astonishment among the general public by the announcement that electricity, under proper management, and by most easy processes, could supersede the furnace in not a few operations upon metals; and that many operations with metals which could scarcely be entertained under the old condition of things, might be placed in the hands of a child when electricity is employed as an agent.

That quotation from a Dictionary of Arts, Manufactures and Mines published in 1867 gives us a good idea of the radical changes that made apparently silver articles available at relatively inexpensive prices in the second half of the nineteenth century, so that all classes except the very poorest were able to buy them. Today electro-plated pieces would be discarded by many collectors as being merely 'Victoriana'. But many examples can still be found that have a real quality or charm. So we must devote a few paragraphs at least to a study of this revolutionary process.

The successful development of an electric battery by Alessandro Volti in 1800 had made it possible for several inventors to experiment, during the next few years, with electro-metallurgy. Most of these attempts failed when the layers of metal these men managed to deposit temporarily on their appointed bases failed to adhere. Then in 1838 a patent was taken out by George Richards Elkington, in association with O. W. Barratt, that was to protect an entirely new process for covering metals with zinc. Almost certainly a single-cell electric battery was used in this process, though the patent does not actually say so. Elkington and his cousin Henry were thriving manufacturers of small gold, gilt and silver articles, and it is clear that the partners' ultimate aim was the plating of cheap, easily saleable pieces with thin layers of more precious metals.

By December 1839 Elkington was writing letters which show that he was ready to use a completely new method of depositing silver on cheaper metals. Then early in the following year he established publicly that he had achieved what we would probably call nowadays his 'breakthrough'. Helped by a Mr. John Wright, a surgeon from Birmingham, who had been experimenting with various electrolytic processes, he had evolved a technique that was eventually to make the laborious methods of the Sheffield Plate workers completely obsolete. On a base fabricated from any suitable, easily formed cheap metal he was able to deposit, by electrolytic means, a perfectly even layer of silver of any desired thickness. And this layer of silver would stay securely in place under all normally foreseeable domestic circumstances.

During the next few years, the old Sheffield Plate technique was used to produce the principal components of most large silver-plated pieces—those, in fact, that could not be accommodated in the plating vats available at that time—only the smaller components such as handles and spouts being plated electrolytically. By the time of the Great Exhibition of 1851, several manufacturing companies, working under licences granted by Elkingtons, were able to produce and to exhibit large and entirely electro-plated pieces that seem (to many present-day eyes) to be over-ornate to the point of being actually repulsive. At first the Jury at the Exhibition were less than fulsome, recording their desire to 'guard against being considered as expressing an opinion on the merit of the application of the electro-process of *silver* plating to objects of domestic use. They desire only to commend the artistic application of this discovery, to which alone they are inclined to think it adapted.'

Ten years later the authorities were completely sold on the Wright–Elkington process:

> There is no limit to the art which may be employed in the production of plated goods by the new process of electro-deposit, and for articles in daily use it is now found to be quite as durable as the old process. It now possesses this great advantage, that if after long use the silver should be worn away in some prominent parts, the article being composed of German silver or white metal, the unsightliness of copper is avoided.

Unlike the pieces made by the old Sheffield Plate method, the new, electronically plated goods could be replated quite readily if, and when, their silver coverings became worn or scratched.

The collector of modest means today may enjoy searching for Victorian and early twentieth-century plated pieces, those in 'E.P.N.S.' (Electro-plated Nickel Steel) being

116

reasonably easy to find. The esteem in which these pieces are generally held, in comparison to that accorded to pieces made completely of silver may, however, be judged from the fact that when an East London man appeared in court recently for operating with a very dangerous gang of country house burglars, it was stated by the Counsel for his defence that his function was 'to tell other gang members the difference between real silver and E.P.N.S., that was all.'

All it may have been, but the Chairman of the Sessions went on to sentence this E.P.N.S. expert to seven years' imprisonment.

CHAPTER FORTY

CLEANING SILVER

Collectors of china and glass have one very real advantage over collectors of fine silver—their treasures need only to be washed and dried occasionally, to be kept in prime, sparkling condition. There is no need to be depressed about silver's tendency to become tarnished, however. Even the pieces in a comparatively large collection can be kept as bright as if they have just been made without the expenditure of an undue amount of time or energy. It is just a matter of understanding the peculiar qualities of the metal and of following certain routines.

First one must know what tarnishing is. Put in the simplest terms, it is a discoloration of the surface of a metal —caused, principally, by the compounds of sulphur that are found in contaminated atmospheres. These sulphurous impurities are mainly produced by the combustion of coal, gas, oil and similar fuels. A hundred years ago, when the chimneys of every town and city were used to send thick columns of foul black smoke into the air in all seasons, even in the highest summer, until the sky was liable to be hidden by a funereal pall, all householders who owned silver had to be prepared to spend a considerable amount of their time combating the ill-effects of this unnatural pollution, or to employ servants to do the cleaning for them. Today, with electricity doing most of the work done previously by 'solid fuels', and with most urban areas designated officially as 'smokeless zones', there is no longer the same tendency for domestic silver to lose its pristine shine and sparkle. Only in houses and flats warmed still by open fires or by paraffin oil-burning heaters is there likely to be any real need for frequent silver-polishing sessions. And even the most dogmatic open-fire addicts can minimise the ill-effects of their smoke on any silver pieces they may be fortunate enough to possess by burning wood logs rather than coal.

Let us think next of the actual change in appearance that may be suffered by a fine piece of old silver exposed, by some mischance, to a polluted atmosphere. (Stored in an air-tight safe, silver will remain bright, even in a murky industrial city.)

First the gleaming surface will become dull, so that it no longer reflects crisply any brightly lighted objects that may be placed near it. Cleaning, at this stage of deterioration, may be only a matter of a quick rub over with a suitable cloth (see below).

Next the dull surface will take on a distinct tinge of orange, yellow, yellow-green or olive. At this stage the silver may call for treatment that is a little more positive (again, see below).

If neglected even beyond this degree of deterioration, the surface that was once silver may gradually become dark grey—veined, usually, as if ferns or feathers have been allowed to decay on it. Then it will become quite black —overlaid, possibly, with a deep plum-coloured sheen. Valuable pieces of old silver that have been stored away for years without any attention turn up occasionally in this state in auction sales in remote places that are beyond the normal range of the hawk-eyed city-based dealer. When this happens there may be an interesting pick-up for an astute local man who has trained himself to look through an unattractive surface patina to the forms that lie beneath.

Silver that is in constant use—and is looked after by kindly hands—seldom or never becomes tarnished. The regular douches in warm soapy water to which it is subjected, followed by the gentlest of rub-downs in soft cloths or towels, are normally sufficient to keep it in a gleaming and extremely attractive state. Put away for a week or two in a dry, smoke-free place, it can be brought back into prime condition by being rubbed over with a soft, impregnated cloth.

'Impregnated'? Yes. You can buy these cloths at almost any household stores, but it is important to choose a kind that is not too abrasive, or the surfaces of your silver will soon be defaced with a multitude of tiny scratches. Some collectors prefer to use jewellers' rouge, in conjunction with the softest cloth they can obtain; others use Goddard's plate powder with a little methylated spirit or methylated spirit-and-water or one of the newer preparations in which a finely ground powder is made up with a suitable liquid to form a ready-to-use cream.

There are, too, tarnish-removing 'dips' that help to bring neglected or stained table silver back quickly into a usable state. (It is necessary, after one of these dips has been used, to wash and polish the silver in the normal way before it is returned to the table.)

Attempts have been made in recent years to remove altogether the need for silver-polishing. A 'long-term' polish can now be obtained that is intended to inhibit or delay the effects of tarnishing. This can be particularly recommended for silver pieces that would not normally be kept bright by regular handling and by the light, routine polishings described above. There is, too, a technique available that involves the application of a thin coat of transparent synthetic resin to the surface of silver, immediately after it has been chemically cleaned and polished. This process is not cheap—the pieces have to be taken to a silversmith, to be sent away for treatment—but it results, normally, in a polish that lasts for many years, if not for a lifetime. Collectors who have to budget carefully sometimes decide to have treated in this way only their most ornate pieces that would take a long time to clean by hand.

CHAPTER FORTY-ONE

PROTECTING A SILVER COLLECTION

'Lay not up for yourselves treasures on earth, where the moth and rust do corrupt, where thieves break through and steal . . .'

Anyone who owns anything valuable these days knows that it may not be possible to go out for an evening's enjoyment without the horrid thought intruding: 'I wonder if everything's all right at home.'

The author of this book was entertained, shortly after he had agreed to write it, by the owner of one of the pleasantest country houses in one of the least visited districts in North-East England. After a hearty dinner that was all the more enjoyable for being served on a table which was plentifully furnished with Georgian silver, he was led by his host towards an unremarkable breakfast room wall, hung with a few relatively commonplace Victorian paintings. The owner of the house moved one of these, turned a key in a socket that it concealed, and drew forward a cunningly concealed door. Behind the door there was a vault which was dark and gloomy because it was lit only by one small heavily barred opening in the thick outer wall. The vault was furnished only with shelves, on which there rested a few small japanned metal chests. Larger chests stood on the floor. The owner of the house leaned down, opened one of these, and took out a splendid William and Mary silver candlestick—

one of a pair for which he had been offered several hundreds of pounds. That little strong-room, so carefully concealed, contained a very valuable collection of silver that had been formed by several generations of the owner's family. Certainly, only an inspired burglar would have guessed what lay behind that unremarkable wall.

To have such a secure hiding-place for a collection of silver is, of course, an unusual advantage. Most people have to keep all but their most valuable pieces on permanent display, locking up only their very best pieces in a domestic fireproof safe or—better—in a specially constructed steel plate safe. (These plate safes tend to be expensive, and they are very heavy and difficult to move, so they are only worth acquiring for exceptionally valuable treasures.) Silver can be kept from getting tarnished while it is in store if some moisture-absorbing silica gel (tied in muslin bags) is left inside the container.

However it is stored, all silver that has any significant value at all should be insured. Normally, an inventory is made by a recognised valuer when the policy is taken out (or it is made by the owner and checked by a valuer). An exceptionally cautious collector will have his or her inventory agreed with the insuring company at this stage, leaving it then with the policy at a bank for safe storage.

CHAPTER FORTY-TWO

SUGGESTIONS FOR FURTHER READING

No one can pretend that collecting silver is a poor man's game. Obviously it isn't. To invest any significant amount of money in any piece of silver on the basis of the scanty information that can be contained in any book as short as this would be a very risky proceeding. (It is intended, after all, as an introduction to the subject, not as an encyclopaedia of precise information.) Fortunately, there are plenty of longer and more fully illustrated books about silver that the inexperienced collector can consult. Among those that the author of this book wishes to recommend particularly are the following:

Peter Wilding, *An Introduction to English Silver* (Art and Technics Limited).

L. G. G. Ramsey (Ed.), *Antique English Silver and Plate* (The Connoisseur).

Bernard Cuzner, N.R.D., *A Silversmith's Manual* (N.A.G. Press Ltd.).

Arthur Hayden (edited and revised by Cyril G. E. Bunt), *Chats on Old Silver* (Ernest Benn Limited).

Mona Curran, *Collecting English Silver* (Arco Publications).

Charles Oman, *English Domestic Silver* (Adam and Charles Black).

Judith Banister, *English Silver* (Paul Hamlyn).

Judith Banister, *English Silver* (Ward, Lock and Company).

Jonathan Stone, *English Silver of the Eighteenth Century* (Cory Adams and Mackay).

J. F. Hayward, *Huguenot Silver in England 1688–1727* (Faber and Faber).

James Henderson, C.B.E., *Silver Collecting for Amateurs* (Frederick Muller Limited).

Patricia Wardle, *Victorian Silver and Silver-plate* (Herbert Jenkins).

And the invaluable

Chaffer's *Handbook to Hall Marks on Gold and Silver Plate*, extended and revised by Cyril G. E. Bunt (William Reeves).

CORGI MINI-BOOKS
REWARD YOUR LEISURE,
INCREASE YOUR PLEASURE

Corgi Mini-Books are the quickest, cheapest,
most fascinating way to acquire a sound grasp
of your chosen subject. Not a word is
wasted. Each sentence entertains as it informs.
Every paragraph is a model of concise
simple explanation.
That is because Corgi hand-pick the authors.
Not only do they know their subject from
A to Z. They also have the unique ability
to hold your interest from start to finish.
You are never bored with a Mini-Book.

To meet growing demand, new titles
are constantly being added to the series.
All are at the same low price.
All represent the biggest value today in
miniature books for your pleasure and profit.

Turn over for list of titles   (2/6 each)

NOW IN THE UNIQUE MINI-BOOK SERIES

CORGI MINI-BOOKS

continued

All these books are available at your local bookshop or newsagent; or can be ordered direct from the publisher. Just tick the titles you want and fill in the form below.

CORGI BOOKS, Cash Sales Department, J. Barnicoat (Falmouth) Ltd., P.O. Box 11, Falmouth, Cornwall.

Please send cheque or postal order. No currency, and allow 6d. per book to cover the cost of postage and packing in U.K., 9d. per copy overseas.

NAME ....

ADDRESS ....

....